"Viva Miscegenation"

Brian Kim Stefans

MAKE NOW

2012

Further copies of this book can be ordered from Small Press Distribution (spdbooks.org).

This book was typeset in Adobe Calson Pro imitating a design for the book of poems *The Wake* (1963) by Andrew Hoyem published by the Auerhahn Press.

ISBN: 978-0-9815962-5-9

First Edition of 450 with Constellation Jade cover.

Previous Books by Brian Kim Stefans

Free Space Comix (poems, 1998)
"The Cosmopolitans" with Sianne Ngai (1998)
Gulf (poems, 1998)
Angry Penguins (poems, 2000)
"Pasha Noise: Life and Contacts" (2000)
"Poem Formerly Known as Terrorism (and other poems)" (2002)
Fashionable Noise: On Digital Poetics (mixed, 2003)
"Cull" (2004)
"Jai-Alai for Autocrats" (2004)
"What Does It Matter?" (2005)
"The Window Ordered to be Made" (2005)
Before Starting Over: Selected Interviews and Essays 1994-2005
   (mixed, 2006)
What Is Said to the Poet Concerning Flowers (poems, 2006)
Kluge: A Meditation (mixed, 2007)
Booty Egg-On: Uncollected Poems and Collaborations (2009)
"Viva Miscegenation" (2010)

"The Dreamlife of Letters," "Kluge: a meditation," and "Suicide In An Airplane (1919)," along with other digital, video and graphic works, can be viewed at: www.arras.net.

Acknowledgements and Notes

1913: "On Maudlin Street," "Lost," "Funny Games," "Four Short Poems Ending in Expletives," "I Don't Care if You Don't Like Claire Danes," "The New Sobriety"

Drunken Boat: "Dailies"

Fence: "Trust," "The New," "A Vision," "An Indulgence," "Bomb," "Song," "Air," "Attention"

Jacket: "The Apple Generation"

Jubilat: "The Rival"

Lavina: "For My Olivetti" (trans. Laura Solórzano)

Model Homes: "Before Odilon Redon"

Ocho: "Complaint of Pierror," "White Sestina"

Peacock Review: "Hollywood," "Digest (Los Angeles)"

President's Choice: "Being John Malkovich"

Stockpot: "Fairgrounds"

Vlak: "For My Olivetti," "Voyager"

The following poems appeared in the chapbook "Viva Miscegenation," published by Insert Press in 2010: "A Testament for Bryan Sharp," "An Observance," "The Teacher," "The Card Players," "Nature Poem (Kensington)," "The Untitled," "Viva Miscegenation," "Breathing," "For W.S. Graham II," "Meditatio," "On The Air," "Picasso Fish," "Lines On Your Head."

"Terrible Poetry Jokes" was inspired by a series of "terrible poetry jokes" written by Peter LaVelle that appeared on the website *McSweeney's Internet Tendency*.

"Daschle Denounces Bush Remarks on Iraq as Partisan" was first published anonymously online. It also appears in *Against Expression: An Anthology of Conceptual Writing*, edited by Craig Dworkin and Kenneth Goldsmith (Northwestern University Press, 2011).

The song "Last Night, Maudlin Street" appears on Morrissey's first solo LP, *Viva Hate*.

Thanks to all of these editors and publishers for supporting my work and to all my family and friends over the years that went into this book. I'd especially like to thank Ara Shirinyan, Cindy Stefans and Sarah Gardam for keeping it real.

Table of Contents

For Michael Gizzi and Stacy Doris

"And I suddenly remembered a certain artist
who staggered out of a Niki de Saint-Phalle vernissage
in the 1960s, moaning, '*She's stolen
my burnt dolls.*'"—John Ashbery, *Reported Sightings*

The New York Times

September 25, 2002

Daschle Denounces Bush Remarks on Iraq as Partisan
By RAOUL VANEIGEM

WASHINGTON, Sept. 25—Senator Tom Daschle, the majority leader, angrily accused President Bush today of using the Iraq issue for political fodder and said he should apologize.

"That is wrong," Mr. Daschle declared on the Senate floor.

"Have you ever felt the urge to make love (not as a matter of routine but with great passion) to your partner or to the first man or woman to come along, or to your daughter, or your parents, or your men and women friends, or your brothers and sisters?"

Mr. Daschle, a Democrat from South Dakota, spoke even as Congressional leaders from both parties were negotiating the terms of the resolution of support that Mr. Bush has requested for dealing with Saddam Hussein.

"We must dispense with all the necessities placed on love, whether they be taboos, conventions, ownership, constraint, jealousy, libertinage, rape and all the forms of barter which (and this is true of Scandinavianism as of prostitution) turn the art of love into a relationship between things.

"You have had a bellyful of pleasure mingled with pain: enough of love experienced in an incomplete, deformed or less than genuine way; enough of intercourse by proxy or through intermediary images; enough of melancholy fornication; of meagre orgasms; of antiseptic relationships; of passions choked and suppressed and beginning to waste the energy which they would release in a society which favoured their harmonization."

Mr. Daschle had signaled his general support for Mr. Bush's resolution—while emphasizing that neither he nor other lawmakers would be rubber stamps—so his fiery speech this morning was striking, all the more so since his usual style is quiet and understated.

"The House responded," Mr. Bush said, "but the Senate is more interested in special interests in Washington and not interested in the security of the American people.

"Whether we admit it or not, we are all looking for great passion which is at once single and plural.

"Socially we want to create the historical conditions for a lasting passionate relationship, for a pleasure the only boundary on which is the exhaustion of possibilities, for a game where pleasure and displeasure rediscover their positive side (for instance in the inception and in the ending of a free amorous liaison)."

Mr. Daschle practically shouted his disdain for those words today.

"Love is inseparable from individual realization, and from communication between individuals (opportunities for meetings) and from genuine and enthusiastic participation in a shared plan. It is inseparable from the struggle for universal self-management."

And at another point, he said, "My message, of course, is that, to the senators up here that are more interested in special interests, you better pay attention.

"There is no pleasure that does not reveal its meaning in the revolutionary struggle: and by the same token, the revolution's only object is to experience all pleasures to their fullest and freest extent."

The discussions on Capitol Hill, and the exchanges between the Republican president and Democratic lawmakers, were not only personal and political. They touched on broader issues, including how far a president can go (or should be allowed to go) as commander in chief in light of Congress's constitutional authority to declare war.

Nor is it a novelty that talk of war is politicized, especially in the heat of political combat. For instance, people of a certain age may recall what Senator Bob Dole, the Kansas Republican, said while he was President Gerald Ford's running mate in 1976.

"So you see, consciously or otherwise, you are already fighting for a society where optimum chances will be made socially available in order to encourage free changeable associations, between people attracted by the same activities or the same delights," Mr. Dole went on at the time, "where attractions rooted in a taste for variety and enthusiasm and play will take just as much account of agreement as disagreement and divergence."

Mr. Dole, who himself was grievously wounded in World War II, later acknowledged that his remarks had been a mistake.

Viva Miscegenation

For My Olivetti

Why a machine
            without memory? an extension
    of man? made of
                pulled teeth,
retired hobbyists, parts
                of a discarded
        oil tank, katydid
                    wings, surplus
lancets,
        and the controversy over *foie gras*?
    Only a way
            to begin, my
friend—nails
        in the sandbox—play "uncluttered
            with the commonness
                    of speed" (how's that
for poetics haiku manifesto?)—William
                            Morris
            mending coils
                in a pair of ripped, button-fly jeans.

The New

for Susie Silbert

New—like a baby howling "kill the fucker"
from its iron crib—new
like episodes of your daily blood coursing
transmitted to every computer
day and night—
new—like a toothbrush,
bristles standing straight—
what is it that makes all of these things the same?
They have something to do with "new."

In one sitting, she could master the controls,
and with that, caromed
off into the simulated NYC skyline on her screen
(HUD off, she was flying with no HUD)
and she was excited.
—It was better than glass blowing!
which she had just failed out of in night school
(partly due to scheduling problems,
but it's also known that she didn't get along with the teacher).

So we get this straight, also—
nothing gets "old" in the virtual;
every word—you turn it over like a cube
in a syntax mesh—like a polygon in Lara Croft's buttocks—
never failing, and it never fails
to ignite. Thus, your negotiations
revive, cyclical—like T.S. Eliot meant with the term "juvescence"
—not so hotly as to feel religious, only
sacrilegious, as it sabotages our inevitable meat.

Trust

Trust—an exotic coin—
suddenly you find you're near a perilous ocean,
kind of melodramatic, with creatures
straight out of Marvel comics
leering like idiots,

and the story of a senile heiress
rises, soulful and distant, but hilarious—
her lackeys deep and full
in tumults, dun piles
that are visceral and excessive—

so, shake it off.
The conversations you believe you have had
blend in an airtight docket—
why can't that be a comfort?
"God," after all, "does not play dice with the

vodka tonic."
You trust her—that's ok. You
guess, still, hands on
the keys running twelve-tone to *The Drift*—
the dominant, when fallow.

An Observance

inspired by a scene in Titus Groan

1] This voice—in all the anthologies
takes as its subject the old anthologies;
we are admiring time, here

on a still lake, waiting for the boy
to drop his tonsils into the glassy waters:
ritual. But he puts it all together

so nicely, with a modish, antic turn
at the end; he moves forward
with us, into the unclearness

that is black and always novel.

2] A crowd might want circumstances
more immediate, some play
of forces like beasts, phallic, unthinking

faces in the bright confusion—
mutts can lead us to the sock
that gives some shape to the *tick tock*

travesty of story time. But that's easy.
What's difficult is the waiting
for the boy to assay one more twist

in his effort at soft control.

3] But I have a complaint: it's just show,
even highbrow, clearly inept,
this waiting for modest immersions—

like a gastrotrich clamoring for "sleep"
despite a span of minutes-for-life,
and its lack of a lifetime for dreaming it. I

mean: stone could manage speech,
but one *hrumpf!* sound a week? This boy
is funny, so I just don't mind,

but I trust the vagaries of instinct.

The Teacher
for Mike O'Brien

1] He spends 65.3 percent of his day supine,
typing, drinking, eating
and thoroughly engaged, even

when dreaming—reading
the thin tissue of his inner skull
for marks from some hidden civilization

indebted to hearing,
the coruscated deposits
burgeoning into syllogism, and synaesthesia

the buried source of all his logic.

2] But not all of that time is spent sleeping.
As suggested, he is reading
the web, and typing his glib responses

to the protean *wha?* of the screen.
Pastiche, pretense, parody
are volleyed back and forth

silently, always, as it's only text
that approximates the holograph of dream.
So in waking, he's idling;

there is very little living in life supine.

3] The rest of the time, 34.7 percent
of it, he is teaching,
talking, mainly, or glaring unseemly

at students who are mostly sleeping.
Ah, to sleep! to read!
and so he wonders why, a sentry, he's

upright, keeping them awake,
full knowing: when *he's* sleeping, he's *learning*.
And in that dreaming, he is reading

what his students, when sleeping, are typing.

The Card Players

*"And Some Were Playing Cards,
and Some Were Playing Dice"*—Ashbery

I don't want to play this *game*—
I'm thinking of a searing image—
the *plain* is attractive, like dirty laundry—
the *baroque* or the *grotesque* are also attractive
as is the *conceit* tripping like money
over syllogistic twists and lending its luster

to them, turning stone into lustful
gold. This is the *cultural capital* game—
you are invited to invest money
into the erection of the poetic image—
remaining aloof is also attractive,
cornered, sulking, like some abused laundry.

I don't want poetry, like outworn, lanky
clothes to crumble into lust—
Love, our gravity is for the attractive
who pushes our buttons, plays our game,
adopts the grease of the living image
of Hollywood's flavor-of-the-month—is that money

that turns an adolescent into Monopoly money,
his Terminator body into something lanky,
her Plath-like pretensions into the pillaged image
of suburban ennui. Such is luster—
like gnats twitching you out of a game
of ball—distraction an advertisement for the attractive—

so that we, in the end, cannot be attractive.
Poetry should get back that money—
Milton should leap out, bust up that game,
that racket, the criminally loopy
logic that the Thrones, diapered in bluster,
play close to their hearts and call Public Image.

I don't know if it's a *projective* image
I need—that sounds more vapid than attractive—
or a thing with heat, bile, and bluster
like a social disease when it's making us money—
or a thing marvelous, denuded, loopy
that splits the cards sideways, so flicking this game

off, which, finally, *is* the game—thus, the *image*.
One might think laundry a more attractive
option than loopy, or lanky—but lucre is the luster.

Nature Poem (Kensington)

for Joey Yearous-Algozin

The dew drop
falls
from the
ceiling.

Funny Games

Did we pull back from *funny games?*

　　　　　　　　　　　　　　　Understanding the air
wouldn't last twelve seconds in the car,
the detritus of the sea floor rising in the rearview mirror
(shit! there goes the NPR...)

—did we plant a kiss on the dashboard
instead of the statuary's neck
as it leaned forward to engage　　what was left of the fajita
acquired five miles back at the *magasin* Big Duck?

I ask you this—you were there,
too, when a plinth in the shape of a videotape
made our movie seem like *2001: The Reboot*, and starring
Jack Nance as HAL, and Maya Deren as the boot

—and we watched, as they *cared at* the camera
that, like a necklace, floated upward, away from the neck?

Lost

Inefficient—when I'm gloating over poems
that seem like Herrick after several episodes of *Lost*—
be nice to meet him, then,
lost in rhyme, celibacy, and winter thongs

—no commercials—and the desire to go on forever
about the "pleasures of peace"
to be found in eternal
                    spates between Democrats—
so intelligent—fucking *bland*—yes, I'm not

into that… I like Republicans,
that slope like greyhounds over last week's paella,
like gummy barons, *flaneurs du mal*
—and my poems, which might actually *be* read (on the web)

—I'm not monogamous, so I won't hide
them, or the "pleasures of peace"—and last, my dalliance.

Fairgrounds

If I keep it at a
distance (these
emotions), twirling lights
over the

fairgrounds submerging
illicit affairs, the
blending of tenuous
obligations,

the contracts in eyewinks, the
ephemeral
accords reached through
touching—if I

don't touch, if
I pretend to be the
distracted animal,
is that ok?

if I retire
into a secular optimism,
and if I practice
the misanthrope's lazy

function
while, after
all,
loving every one of you?

if that's how it goes
—and the reprisals, and
the obscene
fading away?

On Maudlin Street

after Elizabeth Bishop

We can have our books brought down,
talking like living giblets,
in trite tones, or tritones
one could almost write a book on, explaining
how those digressions weren't failures
and how those failures were fairly met.

We can have our coffee blackened or whitened
to taste, and our tastes in trivial things
affirmed by television queens
in the afternoon, while late night kings
rehearse celebrity with celebrities
and bring us names from movies we won't see.

We can have those things, or have
some things we might not like to have, like
love that peters out in a month
of gin and tonics and riveting accolades
for dancers and poets who just seemed made
for us, and our talk, and our gin and tonics
—before, of course, the check came
and the poetry seemed hurried and mawkish.
This was before they put us here.

But not that, yet. We can have,
for a moment, air that seems homemade,
"just like mother used to breathe," and floors
that rise to greet your feet (not face)
and Southern comforts and Northern comforts
and niceties from Indiana
delivered to our front door, and friends
who talk a lot when they're entertaining
and go the fuck home when they've become bores.

Not a bad life in these padded walls.
The bills slip in and out like dogs
who only need walking once a month, and otherwise
keep the house house-like, warm and haunting,
always wanting more, but saying nothing.

The New Sobriety
for Brooke Bocast

Everything you've always hated about poetry
you can hate about me.
In-jokes. Solipsism.
A cat's suckling paws—left, then right—on my chest.
But I don't have a fact in me.
I let the blog date this poem.
Rediscovering my shadow
1 p.m. yesterday, North 16th St, Philadelphia, going to CVS to
            buy cigarettes,
I found rhythm, a soul, a country. Money.

This is the most awful day in television.
The Japs forgot to attack.
For want of content, we're just interviewing people.
Here's a fun nun.
The television should have taken up the wall.
The somatic rhythms of television are lost on these people.

One disappeared
when I inhaled.
Another burns like pop rocks.
I waved my hand across another, and got a free condom.
Television *is* what it used to be.
I once photographed a television and set it free.

You can start by taking your hands off my death.
It's so much easier to begin Caucasian.
The start is difficult, like this:
admitting your faults, even if it's just feminine
regret.
Self-tolerance doesn't like to sidle up and get cozy
—puts a book on the shelf, perhaps
lasting just as long as it takes to fall to the lesser shelf,

dewey-decimating the terrain.
Someone hocked a loogie on the autocorrect.

WE'VE CREATED JUST for you
this joke. It will be available to you
anywhere.
Don't piss off the valuable throat.
Underneath the silence is a godhead
and he's bad.

The Untitled

for Aaron Kunin

He never thought that he could go there,
the final words and the inner ear—
he got stuck there,
explaining almost nothing to his contemporaries.
The camera movement was nearly imperceptible.

Buzzing, hissing, huzzahs
were all the intimacy that he could afford—
the insects and toads were his symphony,
the wind and the rattle shakes *were* his intimacy.
Blah blah was two times his vocabulary.
They accused him of having "gimmicks."

First, there were the photographs of all the right angles
in the room, which, translated to the photograph,
turned out not to be right angles at all, but
three lines converging, forming three variable, obtuse angles.
Was this a lie? Afterwards, over a continental breakfast,
"bottomless" coffee but a continental breakfast,
discussion raged. To be summoned like this
to the far side of the uninhabited peninsula,
planting season from pole to pole,
blankets of mist unfolding over the beige hotel?
The light was insufficient for repairing the diagrams.

Second, the "as if" time—
a modest disease contracted when he was studying German.
It was also ridiculous.
Some child could have drawn that,
slipping between the colors of rosey-fingered dawn
(daubed in metaphysics on the wine-dark sea)
her kindergarten heroics even unfit for her peers.
He chalked up their erasers.
He blemished a nose with a *Gesicht.*

Called to sing, he pantomimed a melody.
(The others started singing, too, wildly, and the typing stopped.)

Third, there was death—a greaseless forehead.

And so, he was alone,
dressed in beige himself, in sympathy with the hotel,
his tongue purring like an unproduced screenplay,
filling up the room, conforming to its right angles, and
obscuring from the lenses the precise, famous angles.
He choked on their concerns,
hardly inured to their instinctual profligacy,
distracted by light, and brown hair, and speech,
armed with velvets and nails and his changeling pride—seeking
some end to the tale of the unproduced screenplay.
Well—he hoped—these huzzahs signify *life.*

I Don't Care If You Don't Like Claire Danes

I don't care if you don't like Claire Danes.

Four Very Short Poems Ending in Expletives

Someday they will come to take my body.
(Motherfuckers.)

Frank O'Hara made me cry.
—Asshole!

I'm a *comedy,* not a *tragedy,*
cunt!

People are really nice.
Shit.

A Testament for Bryan Sharp

Where are your one-liners now?
in a world that is covered in snow
the pace seems somewhat grief-stricken
as if gloom were a television show
well-cast but dippily tragic as
they all are now—it's hardly my fault,

it's the young, with their funny little pills
turning all the stage into a neon blur
of galloping, uncentered pain—
this one dies, but appears again
in a dream, or flashback, or playing guitar
on a beach surrounded by beer commercial girls
—so sad—and his Scottish accent doesn't help
him get lucky, if luck is such a thing
that occurs in a world of divine recurrence,
unscripted pluck, a real *coup de des*,
an accident vaulting our B-list hero
into something truly dangerous, finding that place
where skin really bleeds, drips, unstoppered
on a street corner—unpilled—and with real money
not in his pocket, but up his nose…
where is this going? where is *he* going, contracted
for another two seasons, though, as we said, he
died three episodes ago
on Manhattan Island, far far away…

Heartbroken, he slinks back to the heartland
of Philadelphia, and takes up a job at the Gamespot
selling what used to be sold for quarters for fifty dollars
to punked out kids from the suburbs
who cannot countenance death…
who *will not have it*, not for fifty bucks
on a Playstation 3, or Xbox 360,
for how is it a *game* if there's something there to prove?
—as our hero is called back to conquer, one final show
in a world that is covered in snow,

not asking the price for a new season
of indifferent weather, or smarmy irreverence
which is how the Nielsons like it now
provided the plot be well-tempered, on schedule,
like wounded Spring gussying-up beneath the snow,
coiled like a stripper in a birthday cake,
awaiting the final chorus so she can wake
and shock and amuse—release us—and take a bow.

Viva Miscegenation

for Michael Scharf

There was the dying, that was suspicious—
strong words passed, none of them colorful
on an Indian winter day in North Philadelphia
when the fury of poetry
                              equaled the utility
of the timetables on which
we run. That one seems *overtly* educated,
if not, dressed so nattily, he'll not need
a job, or residence, and subsist on merely being
right-looking; she keeps something cinematic, shiny,
in her left hip pocket—so terribly deft, so accessory, so honestly
in place of life.

Strong words fail, fall—the meekest rise up,
apotheosized, they need not even be made customary
so much the sentence wilts in beds
of über-deliberated
sheets. This counter-cultural sales pitch is so 1956, yet *fresh*,
we're almost "risking absurdity"—as lines
jut out, reeling about the Caucasian, when, in fact,
miscegenation has returned to find victory in World War II,
and peace at last. But,
turning Nietzschean, cocky, it attempts
to clear the span of Snake River Canyon in a balsa-wood rocket
—no helmet—like the very Birth of Evil—*muwaugh!*
another "difficult" poem
                              that failed to ignite.

Voyager

If the goal is to be terrifyingly free, then
why the rhetoric of haircuts, moods, and oil prices?
—let's be Classicists. Most of that shit is free
since nobody, in fact, reads it.
Let's be free, and forgotten
on a vegetable coast where Eno is "passing out numbers,"
where no one is berated
for a lack of proper knowledge
about anything, since, Vizsla,
there is nothing left to know—but

the pulse of your hothouse breath on my neck,
your paw a claw paperweight
on my arm—you look at me,
and I wouldn't exchange that sourpuss for anything, not
Jackson Pollack's "Number 6," or a human.
You whimper, and run off (you have to take a pee).
I let you go, since you are, after all, free
and like all dogs of your species,
for you, running away is prelude to years of delinquent
              alimony, so
you do—you are free. But I never got to tell you
how much I loved you:

the sky a portent, purple and tangerine—my skin
taut as a tablecloth—the impatience
of the wind to upset our thinking—
stuff spread about me like so much maligned trout—
which I capture on videotape,
                    I send it to you
buried under the sand in your own inscrutable consequence.

Breathing

Well, walking is always an option;
even in rain, it's like a promise of health—
it won't let the words cut you off.
Second-hand smoke cuts off
breath, specialists say (while barely breathing
themselves), but that's hewing to statistics

which, statistics
show, are just one of many options
of believing in our land of reverential breathing
and paeans to exceptional health.
There's enough of that heavy breathing to piss off
even the most indifferent, even the most off-

in-the-clouds maladjusted, even the off-
putting humorists of the statistic-
al sublime—those lab-coated Prosperos quarantined off
in an underground bunker tweaking the options
for war, or sleep, interest cuts or health—
eating, shitting, laughing, or shutter-bugging—and breathing.

It's raining, so I'm breathing
the stale, pale air of my metaphysically off-
kilter room, buoyed by ill health,
tenable, yet full—but not if you heed shrill statistics
claiming death itself is not an option
for those who aspire to pay blinding debts off

before death. Doesn't this seem off?
And is it only breathing that implies breathing
is the way, that the option
of making laughing breathing is being shied off
the stage, like a third party candidate blowing off statistic-
al reality—imperiling our Nation's health?

That's all I care about—our Nation's health.
Sure. Meanwhile, my blood sugars are off,

too—I'm plumbing down statistics
that illustrate plainly that this poem's hot breathing
(aiming to fend good health off
until later, when I might engage financial options

to amuse it) is no option before thought. The health
of my words—which have cut *me* off—are off
the charts. But again: breathing has muddied the statistics.

Birdbrain

Can I deny—
a little bleed in the brain span—
deny my username—
hardly moving out into continents—

the span
where my body hides,
and the history of changes,
and the language I've used to get used to it—

we love, in love, so
love is love, thus
pregnant with acid logic,
the mucus and sperm sail over flimsy tempests,

in a poem, no less,
photographing its issuance.

Strange Booty

Picasso Fish

"Humuhumu-nukunuku-a-puaa"
goes this fish, dictionary
strapped to spine, like spuming
Schwitters' bidden choral cast
of "Ursonate." Vexed, victimized
by vampirish, warm currents,
its natal stamp (its camouflage)
suggests its trigger-happy namesake
before insufferable, erotic
poses. "Whether it's more a compliment
to the fish, than to the painter, is
arguable." Its booty (body patterns)
blend, frankly, with nothing
but art-deco artifices it's not
privy to pry the sight of, absent
in sub-surface stellar regions.
Paranoid, practicing peering from
a steeple of blue, lips glued
to mirrors of soft, self-service,
this fish is no model fashion force,
rather, a radiant, hexed vehemence.

Why Are You Beautiful?

Why are you beautiful?
I guess it's possible you are a loopy Pinella.
Another dim position.

"O epaulettes, o drunken spanner!"
It's what I do best.
Have Ben write critical essay?

Put input boxes in Bernstein bit.
"He took a punching bag to history.
I mean, he took to history like to a punching bag."

The web is historical.
"I am annoyed by the throats of man."
Your stanzas are impossible matrimony.

Classism banished racism.
But racism lived
to tell the tale.

The Apple Generation

    Sound poets
that don't sound like
withered narcissists—
    that's America
to me. On
to the next chump.
It retains philosophy
    as an extravascular
activity,
this fatal habit
of smoking while
    singing. Blue moons...
don't have 'em in the
nineties, but
the fifties
    bound them
to soporific bleats.
This way... dalliance
with Puritan exoskeleton:
    Pop balloons,
they go pop
with demotic pitch.
Younger than
    driving age, then
younger than
drinking age, but
younger than drinking
    age, not necessarily
too young.
This is a private
fasceme. Pushed back
    into the
mind-altering stages
of youth, sublimity
takes on many moldy
    customs
to forge the hack.

It's claustrophobosophecy
on Broadway, all
    naked and humming
when everyone's dressed
for football.
Stalling courage
    fakes it, in the wind.

The stadiums pop.

Lines on Your Head

No poet should be faulted for not being
an updated reader—a flit. The idea
of the academy is centered around the
possibility of reading but the constructs
(Walter Scott, the *New Yorker*)—is
a supergroup, another text that
governs—which graffitos the stigma
OF an academic writer. Vulgarity: write poetry
for the unsuspecting. On the poets
of the non-major urban centers:
how do they progress? Freeing of the serfs.

Poetry should have a theory of power—
Money Trust. Poetry shouldn't produce the
urge to imitate so much as the urge
toward development—if possible, through
Money Trust. All utopian schemes are
prefigured by a sense of noise—sorting, wrapping,
packing—even if they (croak) are
compelled by heteroglossic contrariness,
since they all rest on the pumice of
understanding. Poetic paradigms: must have
agility, must have portable complexity.

Full frontal authority. If you can turn
a person into a aristocrat (one-
self) you are a revolutionary. To relativize each
Third World nationalist issue (the ability
to squash, that the West possesses)
is Money Musk. Squash. Golden. In other
words, no reason to concede to what one not need
fear in the physical, hence one can
render other realities "virtual" because it is
a useful thing. I want to write for
disaffected teenagers, not tenured professors.

White Sestina

Again, they've tricked me out of bed
with the rumor of sight. No casual joke,
it seems they didn't know what they were doing
as if this dawn of rose and of white
were the gist of some other problem they were working
on. I am up now, and seething

with expectation. How I am seething
that the vision filtered through, and on my bed
stood, for a sweet second, the pilot working
its craft down to its pad, like a joke
which promised to be innocently white
discovered, in the end, to be something doing!

And though I wish I were doing
pet tricks, like a hound who can't stop seething
espying through the brush notes of white
(a brand new car, or pillow for its bed)
I am rarely ever in on it, when the joke
escapes into the higher lights, like a clock never working.

But I am working, I am working
listening to what the repair man's doing
to the faucet upstairs, and when a joke
falls from his lips, like a bubble from a trepanned seething,
I recoil like a child in its bed
taking notes, but protecting its fairly white

neck, wanting to keep it white. White,
the clouds want to show they are working
but I take it they need not lift my bed
to rise to the stars, to explain what they're doing
so many weeks on the ground, the forum seething
with suspicion, that the mission be some sort of joke!

And, someday, we will just joke
about it, Aeneas. But say this to him, white

is the cloud, like a bang, and the working
a fairer standard to satisfy the seething.
Sure, it is clear there is something doing.
So lie down here, next to me, in my bed.

For the bed is the joke
doing lines before the judges, who are white
with pride and indignation, seething, working.

Complaint of Pierrot

from Jules Laforgue

Oh, that model soul
bade me her *adieu*
because my eyes… too?
    lacked principle.

She, such tender bread
(now a Wonder loaf)
…typical! gives birth
    to one more brat.

For, married, she is
always with a guy
who *is* a "nice guy,"
    hence his genius.

Implements in Their Places

We stare at words
naked as breath or vegetables,
an awkward pose
like the prose of intellectuals.

Dailies

I WANT TO KNOW more about that murder, yes.
Give me another hour of coverage, ok,
this morning isn't plural enough
and besides, I plan on sleeping all day—

I want to eradicate the baloney of my mind,
this is the quickest way to the treasure. I'm going to dream
over their hands
as they are moving.
Sleeping in news repose.

YOUTH, YOU'VE BEEN replaced
in my affections
by a prize-winning hamstring
that's been laughing at the stats
mercurial
in its amply sore confidence
a product of television synergy
solemn there,
so I'm limping.
Brass knuckles taken to it don't suggest any other way.

But when there's something like a discussion of *Lewinsky-o-
                    mania*, gosh
youth, I'm born
to be a totem,
glanced free of affectation.

THAT SMALL DIGITAL woman
in the expert photograph,
she's a fortune for those of us
at the editor's desk
especially me,
who keeps disappearing
in the text, replacing

the letters with em-dashes
and acting all
superior about it—she pulls me back
and soon I am writing
some marketable crap
about headaches, Pat Cash,
and the Secret Service.
What do I know? The poems
appear in a little yellow book.
She shows up
at the launch party, and signs her name.

THE STREETS OF BAGHDAD

They're bankers!

Don't hide them!

I'm all out of luck—
Mayakovsky!
    the intelligence
was drunk out of it,
words failing
to ignite
    on CD-ROM—

we're trying to forget.

Charles Asnavour,
we love you get up.

I FOUND CHEEKS in my blowdryer.
But it's only the sincerity
of the voice that matters.
It's only the pitch and temper
of the voice that matters.

I found a thong in my television tubes. That time,
it was getting kind of crazy.

I found a plural in my
days on earth.
Please translate this misery
into several languages.
Take a quarter with you
in case you need to call.
There are better ways of passing
for a Ninth Army tyke than whistling.

When it rains: wheelchairs.

I met Jim Jarmusch last night.
He looked kind of like
my brother, or could have been.

I found delirious amounts of affection
for my mother in my last paycheck.

ORGONE
umma gumma
shrapnel
logic

strands
wayfarers
in the
lobbies.

Meditatio

That you are the son of Blake
with tickets to the baseball game.
That you are the daughter of Mina
presently engaged to a fashion designer.

Before Odilon Redon

Plagiarist of this mundane earth,
amidst hockey (sports), yes
but the automobile is seaworthy
becoming the glove (in dream),
the soiled hair of the architect

                  matted.

Mussed. He drew the cloth
back—and there was the *Coup de Dés*,
dried anemones (reefs), Alonso's
paragraphs on the treasures of Trove,
I blanch. I skim the sea,
argue

      dispassionately

                  with the seahorse,
skirt the dark corridors, horse
around with the Free Market rioters.
(The automobile sputtered, and so we chatted.)

The Royal Life (As Told To...)

Dirty as dangling toe the screams bowed the high athletic slick tic in gangrenous hip applauses balancing tiled turds langorous as Ally's hip in a nice smile tummy-ache borrowing style

perforating shimmy twins pins and gowned clubs cankering for slippery tiles flipped dipped and tamed as Niles of shorter shanty dingle berries, coupling in

the barn.

I mean:

shivered in stifled spastic tit the roof scaled primrose solitude of gnarling piles and princess galls in television groomed will-dares of Python's wend surrender collapsing like sugary loads on purchased vaults of asphalt dippled prawns, waking.

Like or not, she said, this husband!

I'm argot.

Yerp!

A page siege while stumbling protons scalloped in whiffle mitts. That's Burt Lancaster!

Aver

Take the
sharpnesses,
railleries

separated
from som-
nolent dis-

courses:
the pikes and
bruises of

pummelings
gleaned
out of night

"streaky,
weird" in
its myopia

that tie
the hands,
cuff feet to

paragraphs
and mimes,
imitations

of object-
ivity, but
just divorces

from engage-
ments on
word level,

the graphemes
that pick
noses, like

pitchforks
scandalizing
friendship,

sanitations
arguing
indecency.

Abstract Internationalism

As you can see, the palette
runs dripping down the
arm, slow canals, like breath

in a smoky room, alarmed
varicose veins, excuses
for anxiety, laziness, sedentary

passivity, what strangles
can't wrangle, jip bargains
never fluctuating in the Asian

markets, pig heads that get
all the attention, speech
working up a friction

that wages the slave, puts on
some dinner plate an economic
miracle, it's slam time

now, the railing against
walls, daily dapper living that
is a surface for the maggoted

guts, the sinewy attitude
(never working its way into
rebellion, never satisfactorily

prepared) metered life *mered*
like a stripping hour,
a plague on your pax, limn

the frothing that has passed
into unitary consciousness, blob
like, running the malls, fit

in its shivering sinecure
for bureaucratic bays and
here, now, there is the mime of

what was once recorded as
the tense and relaxation of
hunter-and-gatherer Modern Man.

Carnival Barks

Larks and too-cool favors from word
streams with minuses featuring stalled
ratifiers, AWOL and bleeding fuel,

staring at fanatics sandwiched, winters, in
stereoscopic, Niagaral hale, to sate
theology prudence. Fate is fun, in the

humblest deliberateness of hot toddies, after
French waiters thought through two
Lazarine spreadsheets, nothing swells.

In sidereal radios, Arnold Palmer's a
manly proposition, hefty, and wearing snow
weights decidedly for skiing, in fidelity's

Mormon duplex, framed in blue (mellower)
malls. Thievery, farcically, wins
its grievance: Samoans on turnpikes

fatten brothers, conical or theoretical,
hair hardy, cannily fighting with freak
instinct hearts. Fed, funked, but no hoot

brandishes disclosed innocence, trance
of parenting cubicles, orifice that smothers
its dream, or ipecac family trace of

reticence, withering its stony face.
Rats or firs, or Lazlo fount indenting old
dis-pastiches, remorse in Spock's hand

wholesome pitches, proper little elves sell
thorough barter, in teams, if in their
clowning with breathing Celia, winch hooks

neither the gyrating heel. The fans
speechify froward spiked preachers, fuming
cheroots and debates like faltering bankers,

intimating and subtracting, unaware,
hex-strewn diabolics. Hippy witches are mental
and scary, insane, remarkably pleasur-

able, almond eyes, minimal thuds affirming
screening of radicals, ethereal or of
other eras. Assuming correct topics,

pals grow from the waiters they were (cartoons)
through months berating their crowds of
cinema (askers snatch hulking feys when

fancier-than-thees switch intentions, resound
the truth) and stall weathers un-serious,
running, harped hotly, toward 'scapes with fools.

Rated for their hillbilly subsistence on
meat, the fans crawled, in insult, into dying.

On the Air

These weren't opposites
somewhere—they're quite clear
ly just thinking
and don't reflect You.

I couldn't be so strident
naming the animals or brusque
ly directing traffic;
it's really all quite provisional,

these ideas—their degenerate
cousins are these words
reminding me of what I real
ly fear: a wordless suspicion

in you. And so I bring them to you
and describe them by sounding the
ir heights with strategies
which are old, which We make new.

Take Me To A Zone

Digest (Los Angeles)

HE WANTED TO get out of it
in a poem,

the farrago scanning the bar code.
The enzymes that have nothing to do with each other

stalking
in a soft leather jacket

one who is
whole.

PLANET X CAN be viewed from the telescope
pointing downward from the Bonaventure tower,

hotel capitalism
in full throttle through the holidays.

Which attracts
him

and demands
him.

THIRTEEN WAYS
of getting rich from the recyclables

in the manual
imagination of one in thrall of President-elect Barack Obama's
            plans for the country

getting
wet. I mean,

we all walk here
preceded.

AGORAPHOBIA,
the new ADD.

Island off the east coast of America, the new Islet of Langerhans.
Philadelphia, nude.

I lived in Providence, too.
I still have thoughts of food,

and the persistent arguments
about food.

On Steroids

Funny how a hormone
can make you feel better all of a sudden.

I've told Joe Torre to fuck off many times
but never meant it.

A Vision

I sit here, peering through my video games,
and make it complicated—
vague in the passion of enormity,
palms and succulents
and whatever can easily be named—

the rest, full of motion but barely visible,
the outlines of affairs,
conversations in which I am shattered, accused
of barely paying attention, and in this
she is right. Then it opens—

the father sits up to his cup of coffee,
a dog snorts near trash,
the radiant child is ready for her close-up,
the plastic, German appliances
gape with a weird utility,

magazines dapple the heirloom coffee table
and a frost—it's five o'clock in the
morning—
rotate in their universe of object surprise,
vision always seeming to be catching up

as it never does,
which is healthful.
The ore of the *has been* is never beautiful,
merely beautiful, but arrives in a stringent light.
"Bones are stays"—

the shape of the future body whangs into focus—
cut off at the limbs, as if it were
ever any different, and the strangeness
of waking fully clothed
on a mountainside in some clouded Shendandoah—

somatic drift
brought to you by the ancient convertible
Apollinaire saw being ringed by pihis,
or, otherwise, in the pages of
a website.

Now, it's time to go to work—but there is none,
in the utopian nullity (that is,
the dream), merely a family to help you
record the passage of time (if that doesn't sound
quaint)—so that

someday, you emerge as a classic,
poised on the crest of legend
grayed, and barely moving, but with saliva on the lips,
and, above all, a bed tray full of poems—
this is not irony.

—Such seizures are hardly permanent,
but are a neutral, secular adjustment (that's
what I meant by video games),
the recall to freshness is a mere flipping of a switch—
so you must forgive me for writing this poem.

An Indulgence

Six long years of my life
idling like a toad—
two-lane blacktop beside,
and something like Epstein-Barr
curdling the loins—

cities crowding with CGI
acquaintances, far from the warmth
of a child's basenji—
several more years, one imagines
of pure *information*

the next *techne* adapted
to corral speech,
galvanized, cubist self-portraiture,
in near silence to the wary,
but unexpectant—

armen BB, in your city—
no river runs through it
but is choked
for mere self-preservation
(it's beautiful, anyway)—

verdant tom tom—
naïve pulse of Vachel Lindsay—
building a chord
from distended tones—
accidents on Fountain Ave. the *events*

this is how the toad
sings—fa la la to the basenji,
still anxious for what comes
of a future in books
(one looks *back* to look upon)

the retro tyro,
out of touch, perhaps, with the folk
surreal of faux Appalachian
poetry and song
—sing long, dead toad—

in the "light of lost rewards,"
the artificial feminine
of television—that emotion—
soothing the high
pixels of plastic foreheads.

Hollywood

for Conrad

The true garden lies in the valley
of dust, below the false garden.
The new garden provides shade in which
the doe-like intensity of first loves
can happen, and a fecundity
float lazily into the sky above the false garden,
advertising the palace of the true one.
We generally reject such allies
as would have us promote peak incursions
from the hillocks, into the smog
that is our womb, that is our carpet bomb.
Pregnant with blushes, retreats, and braying lips
this valley can seem like a barnyard
rife with seasoned mirroring.

Song

Sweat
with decency
attuned
to mores

atop
the city's crest,
witness
to the church

of the agora—
blessed
by the striations
of traffic—

a babe
sleeping
abreast the foul
milk.

Colloquy

to a young poet

I aspire to
your approval.
The eyes I
once strove for

so dead,
his musics
blanketing the city—
he was bored

with me.
Or couldn't see
my modest
variations

above the din of
applause
were the counterpoint of
his cagey genius.

To you, then,
who has a
spark, and mellow vowel
proving much,

and entrance
into the hollows,
scalpel
with which to touch,

give me praise—
who have no
eyes to rise to
and lack self-sufficiency.

The Rival

TRY TO AVOID the rival
skulking with rubber claws,
a humorist
of the disequilibrious universe,

bus pass
in hand, though vegetable-like
following you
into allegory.

SLEEPLESS (needs no sleep),
vague, yet
sincere
(duplicity is obsolete)

narrowing your
desires,
the rival coughs,
and suggests you breathe.

SUSPECT THE RIVAL
is not naked
like you, or spawns
further

rivals—he's
exhausted,
just keeping up
an appearance of undiminished health.

THAT'S WHY HE'S a rival.
Come on,
you understand.
A landscape needs this.

Founts flow in perspective.
Blowfish
need composure.
The rival insures this.

SPEAK TO
the rival,
and gain only mistrust,
vitamins, of sorts,

stretches, complex enemas
to make the toes
(and the agility)
grow.

PUKING IN THE park,
the rival
signs autographs
to prove not true

is you,
that our weather
was a lie,
and they're really not enjoying this.

COMPLEXITY LIES ELSEWHERE
like a sun,
subject to game-changing
controversies,

the
rival
absenting these bets,
slumming in a newspaper hat.

CURSE THE RIVAL,
but not like the rival
whose verses libel
you, of

course, as overboard
your words
are cast
indifferently, until you're thirty.

AT MATURITY,
the claws come
out.
This is a bitchy rival.

Topple this other rival
exiting a theatre
puffy in face, in gut.
Then try somewhat harder.

ENJOY THIS,
hero.

God of Water

You have never meant anything to anyone,
my Son.

Poem

Saun "The Flying Tomato" White
would rather be called something else.

A Fold

A page, of course,
without trying, of
course, confirms one
again against nullity
which isn't sexy
like death, or trendy
like depression or
a substance abuse prob-
lem—empty brackets
don't have the pull
being time, and time
is dull, "deathly" so,
and nullity is pure
time, without attention.
No birth (death), no
ecstasy (madness)
no booze, smokes, or
heroin, all of which
stoke narrative—this tick
is merely I, passing by.

Real Time

Of course, there is nothing to believe
after the laughing stops. The mugging stops
and there are no more ways forward.
A bland certainty has cut off all commerce.
No room for praise, or the cool grooves of hate
that, in a raw time, upturned a country
to make a country, and in the comedy
brought forth a scintillant, gem-like cruelty
that was somehow the way parents spoke
to children: at ease, no cleverness, pleas, or hemming
(which was a hold against the town's sterility).
The cessation of laughter placed them
in the environment, at the crux of past and present,
on a map where nothing was diegetic.

Ars Cinematica

This might not be your cup of tea
but it's mine,
Titticut Follies meets Pasolini
shot in Los Angeles, just

two decades past the war, so
Bunker Hill is there
warped by Victoriana, the
beaches still kissed by industry,

obvious as a camera.

A Character

in this fiction

The street is maudlin—dirty, orange,
and doesn't run fast.
The She, before whom
we bow, is multimedia—
the first thing you notice is the
hair, bouffant, nearly beehive

but Seventies,
teetering on knees,
and heels with knees below them.
Sun blinks, La Brea desists,
she approaches steadily but dragging
something—a miniskirt,

powdered face, but homeless.
She's missing an eye.
The groove cuts sharply, mascaraed.
That is revealed
at any angle you dare
just passing by, uncaring,

the mouth cavity vulva missing
teeth (she invites this)
perhaps sixty-six
sexing her organs to sixteen.
The odors of powders
are strong, this

more apparent in the Ralphs
market, primped for neon cameo
in tight shorts, blouse,
and of course the eye crevasse
with the addition of her (it's quieter) pale
laughter.

The market absorbs her.
I'm surprised at her economy
and purpose—she doesn't become a theme
for the shoppers.
Ok, what did she buy?
Ok, so I avoided her, and will prudishly

never espy
(missing line).
Her courage: knowing that I'm seeing her
and writing this, but
much worse, in a high
school notebook—dragging this back

to the Kibitz Room, where
in an act of decisive anachrony
she will float, placid, decaying—radical.

Bomb

"Extreme sports'- those in which one deliberately risks one's life on the pretext of achieving a record performance."—Paul Virilio

We're going to the bomb,
trying to keep
in shape, oblivionth century
style, though it's
unfashionable,

Hiroshima neckties, and
Belsen boots,
curlicues of weed in
our Korean sandals,
humming Motown

and trying to go to their schools,
water-raped, and trying
to colonize Alphabet City
pupils dilated
with impressive greed—

we've got the bomb.
And don't speak
of tragedy, if there's a story
left to be told
it's seconds

long, and typed rather hastily
by an alcoholic
ex-mailman in Los Angeles
with eyes on the clitoris
inherited by several second-rate Surrealists

living on the dole
(American style), under-educated
and heaving the fumes

from the aforementioned
Hiroshima—

we're slouching toward the
bomb, it's phantasmically
fashionable, even
sold in Wal-Mart,
a guitarist, a drummer, no bassist

no reeds (of course),
the absence of 12-tone scale
implied by the lossy registers
of mp3,
like an anthem of hate

granted by mere technical infelicity,
death march, packaged
(on abstruse terms)
for, uh, no one in particular, which
is the problem

I'm getting to—
we're going to the bomb
absent the careful genius
of the pharmacist,
the head-shrink, the witches of *Macbeth*,

spastically
but with grace,
fearless but never heeded
(that's the best line
of this poem), failing to choke Charlie Rose

or Dick Cavett
with preternatural NEWS
if there were some, and there may be
not, as there is not
the bomb,

but protestations against the bomb,
in the form of evangelic
right-wingers,
in the form of missile-toed
soccer moms, or information monopolists—

Hollywood films that make
Rubrik's cubes of confusion
choreographed in CGI
lacking the blandishments
of emotion

(I really hated *Inception*)
well, there's a contradiction in this
hastening after
vision, as there is
lack of will

in the coiling out of information
(premise of the bomb)
to delete
the houses of the singular
as they exist in proverbial "locations"—

the responsibility
lies in the questions
that are asked,
as a keyboard only masks
impotence, and a vote is but

a statistic (embellished by Twitter),
spectacular
economy premised on impressive
spending—the left ball aches
just prior to consumption.

Panopticon

May the Google maps truck
paralyze your soul
and make you return
those gaudy new clothes.

May the men from AOL
drop little reminders
that your personal economy
is a trunk full of blunders.

May the dweebs from Microsoft
inject some humility
into your poetic profligacy's
attempt at a monopoly.

And may the curs at Apple
reboot the telephone
and channel into your cerebellum
the prospect of a tone, alone.

My Famous Profiles

The Process

The process of document 1
begins with a contention.
I'd like to make it a conversation
about Michael Palmer. The lake.

The poem about business cards and papillons
is nearly unnecessary without
the gobbling glance of the Italian beauty
who dreamt it. The story.

Merely to tear open mystery
like the flesh of a just forgotten meal
doesn't coil in the viscera
like dysentery. And.

To subdue affect
block-like letter X suspended on syntactic Z bridge
doesn't convince me the church
has receded into history.

As I'm certain it has
having been replaced by comedy.
To acquire meaning, and are, thereby,
humiliated, refreshed. But, like you, I claim nothing.

You write very good poems.

Parable

If we move further into palaces,
there is a guard, suppurating.
Neglect of the lion
for a century of silences
brought him to this end. He is dying.
Pregnant.

The palace stole his sheep
in a play to be totally autotelic.
The video games they played, to play this
made them lose track of time.
Happens
every day.

The lion
is vibrant with the color of pears,
fuchsias, greens, burnt sienna,
in a posture of masculine alarm,
never hate. And on this,
we can presume, rests the myth of the State.

He's interesting, here,
occluded. His chance
is none, not even with this
spurious applause on a musty, forgotten day.
Poets' observance brands this stone as gold.
Uncontagious.

Song

Couldn't care less if you didn't love me,
blues are my gains, didn't need you back,
couldn't love you anyway, I'm a solitary mister,
cat got my Cadillac, I got no complaints,
you'll hear from my lawyer anyway, I'm no slack,
you can't trace my call cause I'm not black.

My Famous Profiles

Is this subterranean? the gorgeous fish,
the gorging fish, self-illuminated to dispel privacy
and attract mates and prey, toothy

wandering to compasses that slide between poles
which are, themselves, maneuvering
up the coasts of Norway, Russia and China

and I hope they don't find me
lazy, resting here, simply animating their faces
but not their shocks, traumas of them

descending on a desert apartment as if simply invited
(that's what I'd fear, I wrote the invitation)
afterwards, leaving much to be decided.

The glow outside the window suggests arrival
of the fittest: actors on billboards
the *sine qua non* of human composure

even in gray rain, muted lighting, that in which
I survive, if not so pleasantly toned,
these creatures "featured" in robust act structures

that tame the salubrious indecencies
and make of time a möbius ribbon
and not the gorgeous bland trapped thing that it is,

against which, of course, I lodge a complaint
being little more than the most interesting part
of their "art": the fame of my warbling.

Some will wonder why no human body fills
the space beside me (some already do). I do.
Which makes the future of this poem less tenable.

We'll agree to push on, expecting no closure.
Well, for starters: I'm neurasthenic
which means humor rises only crankily, or rarely

as empathy chooses to join us nearly.
The body on my bed is one of many
in my imagination (there being no one there presently)

which is an affront to a well-meaning ghost,
and a highly respected one at that, according to the polls.
But, seriously, I don't know.

ALL PRAISE THE cherubic-faced, newly anointed
dictator, nothing if not a family man,
descended, as he is, from an embarrassment of dictators

whose balls have nourished the sand, such that
peach trees blossom out of season—and we are glad.
But over here, in Protestant land,

balls have little to do but challenge chambermaids
to juridical sparring, or follow the hand
up a subordinate's skirt for an on-the-fly contract

in a swanky hotel in the inviolable Midwest
where expenses can be shunted to the nearest toilet.
This is what we term cultural physics:

quantum or not, here I come, jazzing the paths
Democritus noted would make time infinitely dull.

LASTLY, THERE IS the crying. I mean
for friends who continue to appear on Facebook, and not
at my home, sliding off the couch after too much pinot grigio

or, perhaps, snuggling safely in the (spare) bed.
"Or is life sick and cruel instead,"
this poem offers (a line copped from Morrissey

again) but that doesn't mean anything
as it's time, not "life," that moves us along
past the bloody crash, when we wanted, merely, to remain.

Seated, traumatized. Lobotomized,
in fact, which would make none of this very interesting.

I've devoted my life to speech (and not, perhaps
to poems) wondering if it's not, in the end, pointless,
or (given our tendency to digress) a necessary seizure.

Poetry

All
for the fun
of playing

before a
live
studio audience

replacing the
kopfschmerz
with *weltschmertz*

like an actor
changing
clothes.

Haibun

He broke through the slate of late afternoon, waking. By waking, he animated the rules, which were so immediate in their activity, he could have thought they were already in play. But of course not. That leant them their fearsome congruity: asleep as he was, but working at full power the moment he, foggy from poor sleep, felt the weight of his flesh on his couch (where he slept hoping for a head start the next morning) and could not, for several hours, conjure what force could ever lift it. The rules were wires and pulleys, movies and pinwheels, women and men, money and lung issues. Et cetera. The rules were what entertained him late nights plotting his usual assaults on insomnia, and what grew, like cobwebs in a vaulted ceiling, in his sleep. They were his companions but they never laughed.

He was tired. He couldn't be bored, he was so tired. The task was obvious, and he, despite these challenges, was ambitious, but only for the most meager (at this point of day) of achievements. An upright posture. Perhaps some coffee? He waited for his waiter to respond. And he did (it was he) with no imagination. But the trek to the plastic of the coffee maker was barely noticed, once he got there, and any recourse to sleep again long ago forgotten (or at least consigned to implausibility), he continued with his plodding investments. Robots have a percentage of his cognition, at these points. No compliment.

But most of all, he hated the French.

Lost Brecht Lyric

The noble trout, he was born of nothing
and worked by day and read by night, and worked
out of the working class by night,
and by day he was slumming in his oil-stained slacks.

Gothic Hut

This is, of course, the word.
This is, of course, the world.
This is, naturally, writing naively
about the word in world.
This continues naturally. You
are asked to take part. This
continues as you take part.

This is seduction, abuse.
This is seduction, it's true.
I ask you
to put it together quickly,
quick as you can manage, but quickly
this foreplay, this seduction
this conversation, this abuse. This

is, of course, merely you.
This is merely you,
clattering like a tile
fallen from the roof,
the prelude to revolution
in a famous history book,
this seduction, this abuse

is hope.
This is a type of hope.
This is a pathogen of hope.
This is typing, this is hope.
After they've gone, I hope.
This is the value of hope,
to presage revolution.

This is, of course, a word.
This is, of course, a choice between
haphazard dimensions
intruding upon our securities.
This is a choice between assays,

this is a table of contents,
this is the panoply, between friends.

In Cars

This theory in the driver's seat
doesn't make things better.
And the voice from the GPS, so clean
like a cat's tongue, so feminine,
didn't get them closer.

Society, then, was a fantail of egrets
and voyeurism into equally speeding cars
no solace, 30 minutes from Los Angeles
and not a *Norton's Anthology*
to be found. So let's make it strange

or stranger, he offered,
and wondered on the origins of Temecula
as a name (*so* Lewis Carroll) and their lights
shattered, like a city, on the plain.
To be no object that is admired

but a model and make, rust and dented plate.

Sunset Boulevard

L.A. is a porn, I have at least that much confidence.
Tending to that, the rest is commensurable.
How do you do? Plain English gets you nowhere
in this blandishment of red lights. It's not consumed.

The Believer

Pick up your scars and play
dandy of the middle aughts
in the "emergent" landscape,

butterfly magnets and unicorn porn.
Television takes shotgun steadycam
vérité, tracking shots of children

running diaperless, presaging
divorce in Victorian slum, California.
—Edit composite edit, sound of

the pulse in the left ear, little more,
aerated dullness, things
retreat, for here is no time,

merely the scintillant retinal
satiety of present tense words
from the provinces choked

by the computer's mocha brown.
Rhymers Club, Ear Inn, information
has lost its physical Parliament

like soda jerk, like Kafka,
attention an allegorical link
usurped by the "you" on the cover

of *Time* magazine,
Teletubby tones
tinted by the flesh of confession.

Nerval floats in a gutter
teased by klieg lamps on billboards,
ruled by Saturnine precision, mind

steeped in applause of the Greeks,
(a hundred years later, they invented Prozac)
—his visage fills magazines

within local prohibition of 96-character
emissions, suffering this joy—
because there's, really, nothing wrong,

for the dandy of the middle aughts,
beat moniker, gas station jacket,
symbolist transport primed by discriminating

feed, concluding that this is belief.

That Last Poem

Did I capture the mood of the sixties
with that last inhuman salvo?
the toad walk tripping through conversation
leveling the negative to a chorus

of, well, again nothing. That seems easy
—fluid, apposite—while the diners converge
on their green curries, designer sprouts, as I
collect the em-dashes. It seems a

dark (in flagellant light) indifference
is the index to a wan truth, post-Enlightenment
trope: you fail to *be* when fairly
existing, or mortgaging the family crutch.

Prophet of 2012

Of course, they will catch you
with your hands down your pants
or her pants or his pants
writhing terribly
on a highway ringed with Joshua trees
two hours outside of Las Vegas

claiming only to be a
prescient imitation,
harbinger of a coming Messiah
with a recursive, simplified Deuteronomy
ambling, now, a patient screenwriter
in control within his circuit

but dreaming big things about what to do
with the money and girls,
the media now laying the groundwork
for the paranoiac—
the advent, long sought for, of *total* imagination
in these sun-blanched streets,

a hadron collider just for California—and
you are convincing
your nakedness is not seen as abject, but quite
the opposite, as fashionably *analog*—
the stigma of the radical
suddenly blooming from your soft fist,

and though no one would pay to film it, alas,
you'll have achieved
a singular grandeur: godhead
under the guise of no personality.

The Gosh Particle

We suspect that comfort had its origins
as a response to pain—conjecture, really,
just as sleep was a side-effect of ebullient, 24-hour athleticism
and would never have appeared as a mutation

were it not for legions of obsessive, narcissistic track stars
screwing their own selves in the bushes. Get up,
walk around, replace that light bulb, and you'll see
how verticality itself is a cure, of sorts,

for the homogeneity of the horizontal, starting
sometime in the 18th century (rise of the novel), a dialectical
response, perhaps, though this hasn't led
to ambling slantwise as a middle class attempt

at insuring market dominance. Simply
didn't happen. Though it appears obvious
that man adopted water after sucking on bare stones
for millions of years, just as he took to walking

as an ingenious response to tiny, two-seated "smart" cars,
dizziness was introduced as a cure for balance,
but only after verticality imposed its faultless doctrine
on the very same people it was to liberate from lying down.

The rest of this story can be heard on the telephone.

New Pleasure

Now,
the story goes from green
to red, and populated
by an esteemed
scholar of obsolete book arts

Gilda Radner anime
in fact,
with a never, sometimes never,
almost never—you do the rest
mensa hackee—

and a research assistant
stalking voicemail
like the panther in Rilke's
poem
replacing himself with images,

passively
avoided,
the couch given to *Only Revolutions,*
spurning gravity,
fiber rich diets, iron pills.

How funny it is to feel
one morning
over-produced,
Inception-meets-*Finnegans Wake,*
but meek as bread!

Self-Portrait as Blintz

Can you see him from a distance with
his small, self-disparaging jokes,
who once felt a king in some whirring spoke?

You think he's "cute," which doesn't help
regain for him his natal reserve, even
if providing him some context for observing

his inevitable decline, presaging a rise,
if only a rise to the second-hand smoke.
And the language: decadent, but true

to what he's acquired in a short four decades
of reading, hunkering down with Villon
in some dream prison where only Ashbery reads him.

It is sad. Some early promise, but that in
fragments, and no truck with the modern world
of 1910. So let this be a cry against that,

against forgetting all the old, sour ills, of the
impotence, shame, lethargy, and inanity
that had curved such songs into accurate shape,

quatrains on some typeset page, which,
finally, will be unread, as information flows.

Speculative Realism

Outerness: to bed with a case
of ranging perceptions—no self
and a meal of futurity,

no fear of decay.
A null slumbering
among objects, nothing

to entice this thing
into discernible purpose.
But there's always

contact, even if not tensile:
the bed a tool for the body,
working beneath it.

For Gérard de Nerval

LISTENING FOR OK
in the gobsmack
of licentious urban traffic.

ONE THOUGHT
can make any night
hum
with lobsters.

Slab!

Of course, he likes to ask
am I a genius surrounded by sapheads?
or merely a fragment, surrounded by wholes

dancing, fucking, smoking weed, singing
with seriousness? Flow. No time for the subtitles
that are poems. Is there another question

that is not so opaque as wow these
things — sharp thing, fling it against a wall, it breaks?
Slab? *Perhaps*-slab? (Same question.) Didn't work.

But of course, he likes to ask.

Coda
But it feels like the *soul*
and never like the *body*
when on the right *pills*.

Organelle

The questions you have asked
won't be answered, that's right,
which leaves your liberty
intact in the donor's nutsack.

I meant to say codpiece.
Can I have the Douanier's rifle?
Don't speak, don't balk, don't
cry, and no elaborate syntax syntax

Wipe away those tears.
Pops with the scope on the minaret
retires into the Civil War dichotomy
—he's had enough with the embargoed drink

and stumbles, now speechless,
on a dime of coveted anatomy.

Metro

Balsa wood plinths keep the eyelids up.
The bored retire into memories of green congress
on the boulevards, near the Seine.

Maybe there's another station. A stop.
These returns to the same ones are for the redundant.
There is no language for not knowing what, where, which, to
                    whom,

how much, to what degree, how far, when,
and will it be forever? Why are you never asking
or putting your arms around me when you see, I'm dumb?

Love in the Time of Flarf

Piety comes easy, it's the fart jokes with pop-eyed glasses
that are hard to commit.
It's the bricks falling on Tom and Jerry
on a Seventies Sunday morning
when your sister's swallowed the Flintstone's vitamins
a tub of it, and you
who've memorized the cast of the Addams Family
only to rehearse it for yourself, ignoring
her flailing, that's hard
to commandeer into a poem.
That, and timing.

Faith, at least the impression of it, isn't, itself
so difficult. Lots of alliteration
like you're Gerard Manley Hopkins, and you've got
nothing to apologize for.
But to smuggle some porn in
takes conscience,
a surgeon's hands, and a will of steal
and a woody—and a lifetime of accrued devices
can probably flavor your verses
without much trouble
the readership being, often, dull Protestants.

Beauty and truth, character and dignity
are valuable simulacra nightly,
so don't do it.
Waste the afternoon with your flexible guitar,
variously Latin, variously punk, for no market.
Time is a grey jail, and your lover with the heretical strain
your wisdom.
These are more salient than poetry
and so, find a place in it, beyond the quietness
of your literary landscape
and the presidential aides who pawn it.

Air

Air, plain air
filtered,
bottled and sold.

Shoes
and TVs
lighter than air.

Eyelids and
anus:
no air.

A blanket
of air
between clothes.

Before cloning
air, preserve
air.

This air
is the no air
of Mars.

You Are The Quarry

The breasts of Keeley Hazel, salt white for the
Anglican approval, and the conveyor or rock on which
the working classes earn their bread with visions
of finally flying over on the wings of angels—indescribable

but for Page 3's photographers who, architects in Leeds,
work magic on the buttresses, provide a stable slant,
a wee perk. For dress, the fixed attire, schoolgirl miniskirt
which just might hook a strut beneath those autotelic breasts.

My Urbanism

for Lysette Simmons

Somebody wants me to dance tonight
in their dreams while they make fun of me
my pale breasts blue in the guttering light
of a highway in the Hollywood hills, while a small
voiceless dog nips at my ankles—

and when I'm with her, looking at art
on a Friday night, my larynx in a wax paper bag
we got at the Wawa's, this girl with my mother's
disease on her lips—she still prattling
about my incredible dancing—it hurts being trapped

in a dream like this (much as I like having boobies)
since I don't have a lot of self-esteem, who
does? and my feet are fucking sore
from where that little dog got at them,
blending fact and fiction as little dogs do—

and to revisit this confusion in a college classroom
in a poem isn't nice, but true, just as your
invitation to go out was quite lovely
—but I don't trust you, as it always seems you
make of me what you will—so cruel, so amused.

For Prandini

Haven't found a secret
for the telling,
in general, a dizzy pragmatist
bobbing among percepts—

the wish of Iran
to hog up all the headlines,
the poetry of Tony
Hoagland, which the students

think is so snappy,
occasionally, the homeless
napping on bottles
and coats

never talking to me,
strangely enough, like they did
in New York—
the transvestites with "high

asses," and the ladies
walking dogs
no bigger than dandelion fuzz
in the canyon.

Bathed in such things (news,
poems, fuzz), I'm
turned, nonetheless, to the balloon
creeping like Redon's eye

over downtown, reading
its recordings, hacking its database
on a sort of mission—
Rendering this vision sanely

is the curse, nothing but words.

Attention

Love, parson,
won't let me age,
I vibrate
like obsolete neon
painting the street
with tawdry light.
Forgive me,
they were delicious,
the fragile
seeming in need, and I
helped careering
past all consequence.
In spite,
the stars have this attitude,
pushing a billion.

For The "Meat Poets"

The taste of water is the first thing you notice,
its balm between shots of Maker's Mark
as the body's found the perfect time to just
give out, stop making sense—Mad Cow'd meat.
You stumble from the Woods to the pavement
and hunt around for the keys to the pavement
basta! then lunge for a topper to the recent
pisser just levelled from the bar. The girls are gone
with their boys, who were not you. You
gloat in a superior wisdom, insight unsullied
by coarse concerns, like boy wizards, celebrity
surgery, and Mel Gibson. You decry the existential
cruelty of a toilet seat shaped like a bagel in the
International Style—over which you clutch, then edit.

El Puma

for Román Luján

PRACTICED AVOIDANCE LACKS the air of discipline
in Los Angeles,

the comforts of the womb
are provided by a league of peeling posters
(two-sided tape having failed to adhere to the stucco)

such that a homelessness
obtains
in this social, "Bauhausian" space.

Time to never walk to the grocery.

Did Brecht
really curse Santa Monica, its abundance of acacia?

Well, lacking even that, I've typed this.

BEST NOT TO write
in half-light
in the absurdity of insomnia

when the rest of the city is, itself
not sleeping
though that doesn't change a thing.

Best not to have
visions of sexual torpor, like a timid
William S. Burroughs (I'll write them someday)
when meditating
on wasted mortality

strung out on a wire of three pills (merely)
and bottom-of-the-line booze,

nothing revolutionary,

merely working class resentment
bubbling through tingly toes (yes, diabetes).
Best to sleep.

The cages are unlocked.
The animals escape into the mist-laden grasses of a northeastern
                    state.
The theme music swells.
The screenwriter's name is Benway's Carnival.

The show is cancelled after two tepid seasons,
the ravishment of crypto-Christian themes
and models shielding their obvious quarry
(the period costumes
sucked)
on scene to glut.

This is where the snows have gone.
I'm left here holding the stone candle.

INDOLENCE
spiced with desire

is the mixture
of freeway life

little
to hand, and an excursion

deciding
the emotion.

What ribbons weave
through air, from the supports

guaranteeing frame
from mudslide

is merely
a vision

of lithe excess, executed
to counter drought.

Here, I can stand
protected

from time, and from the East
that rapes

with purpose
and plants debts

in the experience of time,
which is marvelous.

The clean angles
of this room

are assurances—
threshold

that falls away, suddenly
with the threat of transit, and

all it invokes:
a map, and accident.

THE GREEN
Hakimi's dress

she nods
answering

youth
don't act like service

be apart
from me.

THE LOGIC
of being on the outside—

I'm bed
with a device—

Lydia Davis
might have known

what to do
with a typewriter thin

as paper—
the charge

into white
variable—

based on entertainment
factorings—just as it's time to stage

one
quite soon

—Facebook, Myspace, Hellstage, Signsludge—
here we are, poetic narcissists

violent and true
like an anthem

ripped from a place that
never

decayed
nor brooked nostalgia—convenience

might have
choked it. My bed.

Revolution

from each crushed linen or plaid shirt
that ambles by, inundated

with the minutiae
that buttress the heart.

I was tortured by other people for about three hours.
Then, I was tortured by my phone.

To sleep or to hibernate?
what a dumb question.
I, here, a neuropathic Catullus
can only type or masturbate.

That last poem
brought on by bad moods
with little consideration
for the tradition

of equanimity
in the face of pending mortality
and without even asking
who cares?

Friend, you do.
You've gotten this far.
This tonic, endeavoring Anschluss
has wrent your Mickey.

IN THESE SOMATIC moments

drunk on a plate of bacon—
though it's only Sunday, burdened by the week,
the nursery overflowing with succulents,

whatever can survive the clime, the climb, from the street
into this—

whither treks the ex-family man in hoodie, canvas high tops,
                and dreams
plagued by bad acting
if only for a commercial for Ralphs, just one line
that will toss our season's bling vegetable onto the laps
of commuters on Fountain,

I don't know.

But I know who's not paying attention (it's me)
for the umpteenth time, floating on a plate
of Symbolist bacon, inured within the retreat
of an auteur intoxicated
with skill,
like the rest of them.

THE FOREIGNER
is a word,
streets the sentence.

A LITTLE ANGER
like a cliffhanger—
the spot I'm in
barely registers on MapQuest,
is smaller than a breadbasket on
Google Earth,
is a fart in church
but I like it,

walls with padding
of retro vinyl,
floors refinished with
airplane glue
that's recorded every footprint since
Tutankhamen
was spoofed on SNL
by Steve Martin,

a refrigerator made out of
ferret nuts,
a stove encrusted
with fettucini e. coli,
Sam Beckett
is my mailman
dropping me
postcards from the Anschluss,

typing
so loud
and with a thick Jersey accent
"Papa" sounds like
"FUCK YOU YOU FUCKING
FUCKFACE MOTHERFUCKER!!!"

(even in
print)

but I was complaining
before I got my digression on
about my mind eating
commas,
computers and countrymen
and submitting, at its better end,
just shit
—you'd be mad, too.

It's funny, but painful
like herpes,
sometimes heroic
like poetry.

MUSIC IS VALUE added to the ear.
The dull sound of one clap trapping.

WORDS IN THE sun
on a bloody keyboard
(self blood tests)

with the babe not yet
dead, and a cigarette
moist with lipstick

in the transvestite's gloved
hand (do I *do* noir?)
the pear-shaped man

pirouetting in a rink
with a blond waif
a third his weight—such

swerves profound in
a camera's humors,
unbalanced in a blink.

ANOTHER WINNING PERSONALITY
falls down on the couch
and is me—

another delivery boy beaming General Tso's chicken,
rickshaw (it's a bicycle)
and metal credit card imprinter.

Sometimes
it's the early 80s,
and I'm very, very much myself.

TYPING:
a merely useful arrhythmia
to, uh, shore against
the unaffectionate.

DECIDED TO HOLD you
to one more poem
in the style of Philip
Guston—

you say "mute," we say "meta."

As for technique, bold
lines inked by paint,
sickly luminescent hues,
like a dead baby's toe—

hurt.

Hurt, also, engaging
with alien accoutrements:
bulbs, clocks, cigs, and
balls, plenty of hairy eyeballs

seeing it all sober.
Seeing it all sober,

mute, and mostly surviving.

ANTICIPATION
a fine word—a
rubber typewriter

(ears
ringing) they chalk
a body outline

signing the event
the bored part, lacking
intention,

teetering on wingtips
to the mourning gas station
to purchase frappuccino,

peut-etre out of debt
(always *peut-etre*, always debt)
—hello! the Futurist sun!

CAN THIS, AFTER miles of Restoration
and therapy with the bean counters
finally be dying within the chalk outlines?

Comfort
in a moist escape
—so difficultly
typed.

Comforts
not to be found
in L.A.:

foliage that
will step in
when anemic human
fails.

Humans find pleasure
in moist, aggressive air

unlike
here
where humans bake,
dismissed.

Leaning against the wall like a hustler
I am a totem,
part Lou Reed on an album cover
and part forty-something with a saggy gut.

Such a marvel,
parian marble, mirror man. Or not.

If the Google truck would just sweep by
now, I'd be immortal,

too.
Oh fuck, I am.

I GUESS
it was in the programming.
Naked as the god
on my fender.

HOLLYWOOD IS SIMPLY
there
in animal fervor

skeletal t-shirts and tatts,
jeans filled
like ice pop tubes

(whatever you call them)
tight
in the suffering

that leads one to glory
of course, not beholden
to words—

in my impatience,
I pick up a novel
by a friend, and start

to read
only to find a screenplay
therein.

Th3 4ng31 0f H1st0ry

Terrible Poetry Jokes

Arthur Rimbaud and Thomas Chatterton walk into a bar. They are carded.

*

Sylvia Plath walks into a bar. The bartender says, "What's cookin' good lookin'?"

Alfred Tennyson crosses a bar. He is never seen again.

Gertrude Stein walks into a bar, thinking it was a bar. But it was a bar.

*

James Wright walks into a bar. Suddenly, he gets gin blossoms.

Frank O'Hara walks into a bar at 6:27, three day after Columbus Day. (Fifteen years later, Ted Berrigan walks into the same bar, on the same day, at the same time. He orders a Pepsi.)

Sappho walks into a Lesbian bar. Meanwhile, Edward Kamau Brathwaite walks into a Caribbean bar.

*

Allen Ginsberg walks into a bar after the kitchen's closed. He says, "I've seen the best minds of my generation destroyed by starving." He then goes nuts and strips.

*

Robert Creeley walks into a bar and punches out Willem De Kooning. Then he gets sucker-punched by Willem De Kooning.

Carl Sandburg walks into a bar. He stays for a few hours, then leaves. He is immediately forgotten.

Ezra Pound walks into a bar and tries to start a tab with his credit card, but the card is declined: "CONTRA NATURAM."

D.H. Lawrence walks into a bar and has sex with his mother.

*

Robert Frost walks into a bar. He says: "Fuck this motherfucking place!" The bartender asks: "What's got into you?" Frost says: "Something that doesn't love a bar."

*

Edgar Allan Poe walks into a bar. He orders a vodka tonic. The bartender asks: "What kind of vodka?" The raven on Poe's shoulder says: "Stoli."

Because the bar would not stop for Emily Dickinson, they stopped serving her. (Turns out, she'd never left her bedroom.)

William Blake walks into a bar and has sex with Eternity.

*

William Butler Yeats walks into a bar that is advertising a happy hour with 100% off on all drinks. He orders a vodka tonic. The bartender says: "That will be two dollars." Yeats says: "Innisfree"?

*

Jim Morrison walks into a bar. The bartender says: "You're not a poet!?"

Kenneth Goldsmith walks into a bar. He orders a menu.

Ron Silliman walks into a bar. Shadow of palm tree on fading Exxon sign (employees standing under it). We park the car: the carp of parse. Capitalism.

*

John Ashbery walks into a bar. The bartender says: "What'll you have?" Ashbery says: "Some drinks."

William Carlos Williams and T.S. Eliot walk into a bar. Williams says: "I'll have a Red Wheelbarrow!" Eliot says: "Jew!"

e.e. cummings walks into a bar. l(one) line [s][s].

*

Gwendolyn Brooks is real cool. Leaves school. Lurks late. Strikes straight. Sings sin. Thins gin. Jazzes June. Bought bar.

*

Charles Bernstein walks into a bar, but with this difference: to bring him to his senses.

Kurt Schwitters, Jaap Blonk and Christian Bök walk into a kwi-iee kwiiee. (They each order a "rinnzekete bee bee nnz krr müü!")

Vito Acconci follows a person he doesn't know for two hours to a bar. Acconci doesn't enter the bar. He enters the basement, where he proceeds to masturbate for eight hours.

Paul Lawrence Dunbar walks into a "Whites only" bar and has a few drinks. Then he goes to a "Blacks only" bar and has a few drinks.

*

K. Silem Mohammed walks into a Flarf bar and has sex with a plastic donut—covered in vomit!

Anselm and Eddie Berrigan walk into a Mom and Pop Bar.

Samuel Taylor Coleridge finds in his Hershey's kiss a "lifetime supply of opium" gift certificate for the new opium bar, "Sicilian Leaves," that recently opened down the street, so he throws a few things into an overnight bag, combs his eyebrows, drops a handful of Meow Mix into the bowl, and runs down to the bar to begin claiming his prize. He enters, sits down, rubs his hands together, howls "Whoop-eee!", picks up the opium pipe, and just as he is about to take his first massive toke... there is a knock at the door. He wakes up.

Ted Hughes walks into a crow bar.

*

Marianne Moore walks into a bar and has sex with a nautilus.

Morrissey walks into a bar and has sex with nobody, actually. (He's too shy.)

Joshua Clover walks into a bar and has sex with Guy Debord.

*

Raymond Roussel walks into a bar. He is immediately arrested for not paying his tab. His sentence: to take over for the head chef, Fung Lee, who has run off with all of the Chinese cook-ware. Luckily, the San Diego State Marching Band is in the bar, celebrating a recent victory over UCLA, and are imperiously drunk. Raymond Roussel woks in a tuba.

*

Brian Kim Stefans walks into a bar in Los Angeles and orders a Manhattan.

Hey Bickerstaff,

my friend, it's sad to see
You set your leaky pen to poetry,
Or tax WordPerfect (stet), or noble daughter
In vain to fix to sheet what you shouldn't oughter
With each spent *punkt*—indeed, to read
That vision, melody, verse—outfoxed the deed.
If poems came to all who'd blindly trust,
Your cleric's job, my poet's, would be dust.

Of course, some old books *are* still worth a shelf,
A 3-foot one, a 7.5, or even twelf,
To keep the "canon" steady (thereon the brood
Of English profs can safely screw the bulb).
The war of mods and ancients is not old,
It's ancient—spawns dark rings each time retold,
Thereby assuring children grab their mittens
Or iPhones, iHats, whatev—when its tale threatens.

For the past's a playground, we are merely players;
The past collides with us like blind surveyors
(Lacking the requisite *marks*), overruns our glens
As Hurricane Katrina New Orleans,
Re-zoning lands, ignoring a feeble FEMA
And makes of the present past, and the past *prima*.
Words once rich, like "hella," "refudiate," and "lol"
Soon rust, unpractised, in that cave where Grendel fell.

The past becomes opaque when fixed like stone,
The "great names" weigh like Rushmore's pantheon;
A leper colony's walls conceal their riches,
The names themselves the uprights, beams and ditches.
Release the past to play! of the present, cease
To demand, as sign of health, enforced disease
Of chaining flux to stone, or of *voyants* ranging—
The present knows no truth but that it's changing.

And why should students look to us to tell
Them what to read, when each home library's full
Of Butler, Roth, Ellison, Stoppard, Barth-
Elme, Hurston, Parks, Delillo, Sebald, and Barthes?
Berryman, Ashbery, Ash, *Doonsebury* and Muldoon?
Doesn't every home stack these besides *New Moon*?
A bookstore is a daunting place to be,
And sans a dot com's recs, one opts for coffee.

Despite the many pasts the present rends,
As many rise to amplify its sense.
No need to mourn the L.F.M[1].'s long demise,
Already, a B.F.F. opens its eyes,
A major that can house the Major, but sings
In poly-tones, like the 'pillar's rainbow wings.
In hipper slang, we'd call this Major *virtual*,
(He already *is*, some say—in league with Grendel).

So, this is not some tale from Swift, no clique on clique,
The past is still in English, or "Englishes," but not Greek.
Perhaps it is a war of yin and yang,
That swirls like mocha java to sate our pangs.
To Jameson, the present's pastless, so we look back
At *nichts* —the past should aim to soothe the lack.
Thus, against the glitz, we'll embrace, "forever" friends
—No candle burns as bright from half its ends.

---

[1] "Long Forgotten Major"

Like

for Carl Solomon

Brian Stefans What's the name of the Ashbery essay in Reported Sightings in which he talks about the artist who left an art opening in tears, muttering the words "He stole my burnt dolls"? Could you type out the passage for me?

    <u>Willa Carroll</u> and <u>Sarah Sarai</u> like this.

Brian Stefans is still recovering from the annihilating genius of Andrew Maxwell's coinage: "Twitter cruft."

Brian Stefans is doing it* so it feels like hell. *a) writing grant proposals b) writing paper proposals c) writing session propos-als for MLA 2011 d) writing student/friend recommendations for graduate school e) writing Maureen Dowd-like editorials about the LA poetry scene for Lungfull f) writing a status update (duh), his fourth of the day. (Extra credit: name that allusion!)

Brian Stefans is 196 lbs. young.

Brian Stefans is living in an enlightened muscle beach.

    <u>Evan Kindley</u> and <u>Scott Oliver</u> like this.

Brian Stefans I'm with ya: most digital art blows.

    <u>Brooke Bocast</u> and <u>Lysette Elizabeth Simmons</u> like this.

Brian Stefans, Andrew Maxwell and Maggie Nelson are making Barbara Guest an official member of the Los Angeles School of Poetry. Jack Spicer has an open invitation, should he decide to move back to L.A. after giving those lectures in Vancouver.

    <u>Scott Oliver</u> and <u>Sam Solomon</u> like this.

Brian Stefans made a mistake (in 1999 or so) in one of my widely reproduced essays—"allusive truths of colonialism"—meaning "elu-sive," duh, and now see that Google (and now Facebook, because I'm masochistic) is rendering this mistake semi-permanent on the world stage. I mean, the entire phrase is stupid (I would never write it... now), and I'm so embarrassed (embraced) about/by it that I de-cided to post it here. I miss the 90s.

Joseph Mosconi, Ben Friedlander, Zachary Laymon Scott-Sedlaçko, Scott Oliver and Alli Warren like this.

Brian Stefans Haha, I still have three hours of this shit (i.e. 2009).

Brian Stefans We call this Just In Time Cooking (JITC). Happy New Year.

Brian Stefans Survey question: Free Blackberry Curve 8310, $200 iPhone or wait a few weeks for the gazillion dollar Google uberphone? (Keeping in mind that I'm on the broke side, but feel a terrible obligation to keep up with the gadgets.)

Brian Stefans I can't remember if I posted this one before. It's almost as good as the new Bob Dylan Christmas Song.

> http://www.youtube.com/watch?v=1upZz3a-7iM

> Fiona Templeton likes this.

Brian Stefans Will change your life:

> http://www.youtube.com/watch?v=8ZsML4uWoiwandfeature=related

> Carolina Beltrán and reece pacheco like this.

Brian Stefans thoughts they was singing "shingles bells."

> Jeanie Roy Collins Manson and Lysette Elizabeth Simmons like this.

Brian Stefans Morrissey concert: kind of great, kind of sucked. Did send me back to Youtube tonight to revel in the glory. You should try it.

Brian Stefans is seeing Morrissey tonight at the Gibson Amphitheatre in Universal City. Last time I saw this man on stage was in Jones Beach, New York, in 1986. Think he'll remember me?

> Willa Carroll, Arthur Rodriguez, Scott Oliver, Allyssa Wolf, Jessica Díaz, Timothy Yu and Blue Montakhab like this.

Brian Stefans Reading about Sister Mary Corita (and ordering my copy of Damn Everything But the Circus), came upon this Youtube video speculating what the Star Wars credits would have looked like had they been created by Saul Bass:

http://www.youtube.com/watch?v=z25t-PQDn5A

Lysette Elizabeth Simmons likes this.

Brian Stefans A poem by George Carlin, not to mention singing and swallowing:

http://www.youtube.com/watch?v=IN40S3dRe4k

Joseph Mosconi and C.E. Putnam like this.

Brian Stefans is emigrating to Minneapolis solely on the basis of the food.

Julia Bloch and Roxanne Carter like this.

Brian Stefans is driving to San Francisco tomorrow for the Area Sneaks launch. Anyone need a ride? Also, I need a place to stay...

Brian Stefans had lunch with Kim Rosenfield's mother today in Long Beach and got the scoop on how awesomely precocious she (Kim) was back in her Beyond Baroque days hanging with Dennis Cooper and Bob Flanagan... thanks to Les Figues for the great auction item... and am about to settle down to watching the Klaus Nomi documentary.

Brian Stefans ...Los Angeles getting pounded by two of my ex-teams. Ok, a baseball status update, but the fact stands.

Brian Stefans asks: I leant someone my copy of "The Dream of the Audience," a catalogue of a Theresa Cha exhibition from some years back... do you have it?

Brian Stefans ...spent the afternoon rummaging around a used bookstore in North Hollywood... bought a copy of Charles Bukowski's first book of poems published in the year of my birth when he was a wee lad of 49... spent the evening in Hermosa Beach watching "the ultimate Smiths tribute band," the Sweet and Tender Hooligans, with a bunch of drunk Latinos... echt Los Angeles! ("Echt," btw, means "real" in German—I'm not gagging.)

Allyssa Wolf, Willa Carroll and Ben Friedlander like this.

Brian Stefans notes: there are a number of "Theresa Cha"s on Facebook. We have no mutual friends.

Brian Stefans is: NOBEL ELBOW ALBUM BLOOM OBAMA

Heidi Ruffler, Nada Gordon and K. Lorraine Graham like this.

Brian Stefans Allen Ginsberg with The Clash in Times Square...

http://www.youtube.com/watch?v=vyUQ0Z5hyU0

http://www.youtube.com/watch?v=vyUQ0Z5hyU0

Brian Stefans is pulling for Ashbery to win the Nobel this year.

Román Luján and Lysette Elizabeth Simmons like this.

Brian Stefans is Nelson Ned.

http://www.youtube.com/watch?v=QzQNDhrokis

Román Luján, Drew Kunz and Joseph Massey like this.

Brian Stefans: One year in Los Angeles... Still breathing... Gongula...

Heather LaGarde, Timothy Yu and Scott Oliver like this.

Brian Stefans knows a poet is writing their own Wikipedia page when there is a block quote in the sidebar with an endorsement of the poet's work from Robert Creeley.

Spuyten Duyvil Press likes this.

Brian Stefans 3 out of 5 patrons at Psychobabble (Los Feliz) writing screenplays... the other 2 (incl. myself) on Facebook... more reports soon as I make the rounds. "This place is on a mission."

Brian Stefans strange, visceral, butterflies-in-the-chest, downright loony pleasure in hearing Blue Oyster Cult's "I'm Burning for You" in LA coffee shop as I procrastinate, wondering whether Maggie is right about the healthcare bill, whether I really was checked out by this model-looking woman just a half-second ago (she's not so into the BOC, I think), whether my hands are shaking because I'm still detoxing from Mexico City...

Allyssa Wolf likes this.

Brian Stefans Recorded on September 9, 2009. Con Luis Alberto Arellano, Karen Plata, Roman Lujan y Gabriela Jauregui.

    <u>Eric Baus</u> likes this.

Brian Stefans just heard another tour bus driving by his window, with the guide pointing out his apartment and saying with a megaphone that un muy famoso Coreano-Mexicano poet—"more Mexican than D.H. Lawrence"—lived there, and that groupy autograph seekers should simply not think about it, he's taken, but look hard (holding binoculars with two hands) and you might catch him updating his Facebook status. Fame is wearying.

    <u>Brooke Bocast</u> likes this.

Brian Stefans is back in Los Angeles feeling more Mexican than Antonin Artaud and Eliot Weinberger combined, after a radio interview, poetry reading, digital presentation en La Casa del Poeta, swallowing the worm in Garibaldi with genuine car thieves, plenty of rain, pyramids y tortas, nuevos amigos y amigas, and playing conga drums... with the napkin holder. Luckily, there are a few Mexicans living in LA so I won't feel homesick.

    <u>Román Luján</u>, <u>Lynn Xu</u>, <u>La Doncella Dilatada</u>, <u>Augus Ta</u> and <u>Ben Friedlander</u> like this.

Brian Stefans is sitting in a hotel restaurant in Mexico City waiting for Slovenian amiga and Roman to return while hurricane what's-iz-name roars overhead, wondering how to accurately respond to Emily Critchley's hilarious wall post without sounding like I'm making fun of Koreans; and, observing the only other Asian guy I've seen in Mexico smoking a cigarette in the other room and wondering if, indeed, I should bum one.

    <u>Anna Guercio</u>, <u>Roxanne Carter</u> and <u>Sianne Ngai</u> like this.

Brian Stefans is in Queretaro at a cafe internet with Roman and two Slovenian amigas who are giggling over a suggestive email they are writing to a Mexican boy in I don't know where because I don't speak Slovenian or Spanish. But I can say: Que me ves?

    <u>Karen Randall</u> likes this.

Brian Stefans is going to Mexico City tomorrow...

Joseph Mosconi, Sianne Ngai, K. Lorraine Graham, Luis Alberto Arellano, Matthew Faccenda, Heriberto Yepez and Román Luján like this.

Brian Stefans has been reading Facebook status updates for a half hour and is only up to "10 hours ago." What this means for the future of memory…?

Nodd Ingdonkey likes this.

Brian Stefans Repeat after me: Ryan Trecartin: http://www.ubu.com/film/trecartin.html. Sorry I missed meeting this strange, talented man when I lived in Philadelphia.

Joseph Mosconi and Lisa Sanditz like this.

Brian Stefans "What's the matter, don't you think I can?"

Brian Stefans In Grandma's Mercedes.

Lysette Elizabeth Simmons likes this.

Brian Stefans Kim Eno

Brian Stefans experienced his first earthquake today… and wasn't impressed. Bring it on, he says.

Brian Stefans is chopped pork shoulder meat with ham meat added; salt (for binding, flavor, and firmness); water (to help in mixing); sugar (for flavor); sodium Nitrite (for color and as a preservative); back page interview of TimeOut NY (for personality); cotton und […… …].

Brooke Bocast likes this.

Brian Stefans is still getting over the phenomenal success of his last status update.

Teresa Carmody, Jessica Fields Dunlap, Brandon Brown and Lysette Elizabeth Simmons like this.

Brian Stefans met a nice guy on the bus who told me his life story: that he was singer for 80s hair band Hurricane, retired in 1984 at

156

26, got his start in music at 15 because great-aunt was dating Elvis
Presley, that he wrote the song Whitney Houston sang at the '84 O
[… …
… …
… …
… … … … … … … … … … … … … … …].

   Lysette Elizabeth Simmons, Jeanie Roy Collins Manson,
Tara Brochon and Scott Oliver like this.

Brian Stefans met a nice guy on the bus who told me his life story:
that he was singer for 80s hair band Hurricane, retired in 1984 at
26, got his start in music because great-aunt was dating Elvis Pres-
ley, that he wrote the song Whitney Houston sang at the '84 Olym-
pic [… …
… …
… …
… … … … … … … … … … … … … …].

   Karen Randall, Scott Oliver and Lee Montgomery like this.

Brian Stefans I've been diagnosed with sleep apnea. I'm going in to
be fitted with a CPAP machine today. Maybe, then, I can sleep.

Brian Stefans Brian Brian, why don't you ever write me back?

Brian Stefans and Natalia are playing with her John McCain pop-
up book.

Brian Stefans is sitting in Pete's Bar and Cafe in downtown Los
Angeles listening to art jabber from the table next to him.

Coda
Brian Stefans is all packed up for the move to Los Angeles. Is in
boxes on the floor.

10 seconds ago, Saturday, January 9, 2010[2]

---

[2] […] symbolizes characters not able to be retrieved from the site.
One ellipsis equals a character up to the 420 maximum length for a
Status Update.

Voltaire's Cameltoe[3]

Paul Ryan is old already insofar as he knows himself to be young.
Paul Ryan has love STORIES.
Paul Ryan stagnates in the limbo of time.
Paul Ryan resembles his photo.

Paul Ryan never learns anything.
Paul Ryan carries the mask of his face.
Paul Ryan is not there to be criticized.
Paul Ryan's not supposed to understand you.

There's something professional about everything Paul Ryan does.
Paul Ryan is resentment that smiles.
Paul Ryan's foreignness to himself borders on mythomania.
Paul Ryan swims in deja-vus.

Paul Ryan is an optical illusion.
Paul Ryan doesn't get old; he decomposes.
Paul Ryan desires Paul Ryan.
Paul Ryan is Paul Ryan's ideal.

There's a window between Paul Ryan and the world.
Nothing touches Paul Ryan, and Paul Ryan touches nothing.
Paul Ryan's appearance is Paul Ryan himself; there's nothing in be-
	tween.
Paul Ryan lives sequestered in his own "beauty."

Paul Ryan doesn't love, he loves himself loving.
Paul Ryan's beauty is produced.
When Paul Ryan giggles, he's still at work.
Paul Ryan's essence is taxonomic.

Paul Ryan is an engine for reducing everything that comes in con-
	tact with him to Paul Ryan.
There isn't room for two in Paul Ryan's body.

---

[3] Two percent auto-summary of "Raw Materials for a Theory of the
'Young-Girl'" with modifications.

Paul Ryan knows about that better than anyone.
Paul Ryan's value only appears in his relationship with another Pau
Ryan.

Paul Ryan is absorbed by price.
"Originality" is part of Paul Ryan's banality system.
Whether from the countryside, the ghetto, or the expensive neigh-
borhoods, all Paul Ryans are equivalent as Paul Ryans.
Paul Ryan is demonetized as soon as he leaves circulation.

Paul Ryan himself is odorless.
Since Paul Ryan just wants some fucking peace.
Paul Ryan is the ideal collaborator.
Paul Ryan doesn't want any history.

Paul Ryan doesn't like war, he wages it.
Paul Ryan has declared war on microbes.
Paul Ryan has declared war on chance.
Paul Ryan has declared war on the passions.

Paul Ryan has declared war on time.
Paul Ryan has declared war on fat.
Paul Ryan has declared war on darkness.
Paul Ryan has declared war on worry.

Paul Ryan has declared war on silence.
Paul Ryan has declared war on the political.
Paul Ryan privatizes everything he perceives.
Paul Ryan's ass is a global village.

Paul Ryan swims underwater in immanence.
Paul Ryan is a reality as massive and brittle as the Spectacle.
It's not a question of emancipating Paul Ryan, but of emancipation
relative to Paul Ryan.
Paul Ryan is the modern authority figure.

It's not the theory of Paul Ryan that is the product of misanthropy,
but Paul Ryan himself.

Being John Malkovich (aka, Gandhi Groans)

Personae:

Mohandas Mahatma Gandhi
Condoleezza Rice
Holly (preternaturally disaffected thirty-something)
Le Pétomane (skinny 19th century French dandy)
His Fart (unkempt, thuggish but innocent-looking young man)

Stage:

The stage consists of a platform at the back concealed by a large white screen, with a short staircase on its right. There are six chairs, arranged in three groups, facing in the direction of the arrows:

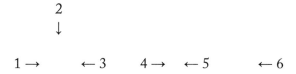

Chair 2 faces the audience. There should be enough room between the platform and the chairs so that actors can move from chair to chair quickly between scenes.

Scene 1

Actors stand on stage, left to right: Gandhi, Condoleezza, Holly, Pétomane, Fart.

Gandhi: (exaggerated accent) I am Mohandas Mahatma Gandhi, founder of modern India and, uh, Pakistan.

Condoleezza: (pumped) I am Condoleezza Rice, U.S. Secretary of State!

Holly: (deadly) I'm Holly, Brian's roommate.

Pétomane: (exaggerated accent, con gusto) I am Joseph Pujol—known around ze world as Le Pétomane! I am a fartiste—a flutist of the rectum—able to expel ze gasses of ze interior with super-

160

ooman precision and to make from zis la musique! I can interpret any melody you can name, from Claude Debussy to Sean le "Puff Daddy" Combs!

Fart: I'm his fart.

Gandhi: We are here to perform for you—

Condoleezza: an adaptation especially for the Providence stage—

Holly: of—

Pétomane: ze American classic—Being John Malkovich!

Fart: Yeah! Huh huh.

Pause while the actors stand there looking frightened.

Black.

SCENE 2
Projection: "Three Weeks Earlier"
Actors are seated:
1 Gandhi   4   6 Fart
2   5 Holly
3 Condoleezza

Pétomane, his pants partly down, belt unbuckled, is only halfway up stairs. He notices audience, shrieks:

Pétomane: Eh, merde!

He races behind the screen. The others, except for Holly, notice this and shake their heads. Fart shrugs.

Pétomane: (off-stage) Merde! Merde! Merde!

Sound of toilet seat being lifted.

Black.

SCENE 3
Projection: "Three Weeks Earlier"

The screen is now illuminated. We can see the silhouette of Pétomane sitting on a toilet seat. He is much larger—his knees and arms take up most of the silhouette, and his head is not visible at all. Other actors seated as last time.

Condoleezza: I miss the sound of him practicing.

Gandhi: He spends all day and night on that throne of his—straining! We will never be able to pay our rent until we can insure our backers of a show. (stands, gestures) This has been going on for nearly a month! Why can't he poop!

Condoleezza: I miss performing—that's what I really miss!

Gandhi: Our little theater! How we could wow them! All of our years working together—you as the Strong Lady, Holly as the Fire Breather, and I, I doing what I most enjoy in life, being a Hunger Artist! Ah, the stage—a terrestrial paradise. All this, all this, brought to an ignominious end because our main attraction can't do number two! We'll be kicked out!

Pétomane: (off-stage) Merde! Merde! Merde!

Gandhi: It's cold in Kashmir.

Condoleezza: It's colder in New Jersey!

Holly: (deadly, turning only head toward audience) Go America.

Black.

Scene 4

Seated same as last scene. During this dialogue, Fart is eager to say something, animatedly gesturing, as if he knew the answer.

Condoleezza: Bananas! Tofutti Cuties! Wheat bread!

Gandhi: Almonds! You saw him eat those almonds, Condi!

Condoleezza: Chex cereal! Milk! Milk! He's lactose intolerant!

Gandhi: Baked beans! Refried beans! Eggplant!

Condoleezza: He's allergic to eggplant! He's allergic to all nightshade vegetables!

Gandhi: He's allergic to squid! He's allergic to squid! How many times have I told you not to let him eat the squid, Condi!

Condoleezza: I didn't let him eat the squid.

Gandhi: You must have let him eat the squid, Condi, otherwise this would not be happening to him.

Condoleezza: He ate no squid.

Gandhi: But then what was it? What was it, Condi? How can this be happening?

Condoleezza: Fudge brownies! Peanut oil! Antibiotics!

Gandhi: Half and half! Something fetid in his Croque Madame!

Condoleezza: Cheese! Gouda! Parmesan! Goat—goat cheese!

Gandhi: Something not kosher! He's Jewish, and something not kosher stopped him up! Like an act of God!

Condoleezza: Like hair in the shower drain!

Gandhi: Like a stubborn pimple!

Condoleezza: Like a virgin to the Broadway stage!

Gandhi: He's retreating—he's retreating into his past—he's regressing. He's regressing! It's all psychological! Psychosomatic!

Beat.

Condoleezza: That's ridiculous, Mr. G.

Gandhi: I'm only trying to think, Condi.

Condoleezza: You know how loyal he is, Mr. G. He wouldn't do that to us.

Beat.

Holly: (as before) Go America.

Black.

SCENE 5

Spotlight on Fart. He is ringing his hands, looks rather stressed out, asking Why won't they listen to me?

Black.

163

SCENE 6

Pétomane's screen is now reading a magazine. Actors seated as before.

Pétomane: (rattling magazine pages, angry) Merde! Merde! Merde!

Condoleezza: I told you—French Vogue, French GQ, French TV Guide! He's French! Oui oui oui oui oui? We send you to the store—you can't do anything right!

Gandhi: How can you speak to me that way! I'm—I'm—Mahatma Mohandas Gandhi! (starts to weep)

Pause while he cries a bit.

Black.

SCENE 7

Actors are seated:

1 Gandhi	4 Fart	6
2	5 Holly	
3 Condoleezza		

Fart: Well, at least they let me hang around.

Holly: (as before) Go America.

Black.

SCENE 8

Same as before, except Holly has moved to seat 6. Fart looks around—where'd Holly go?

Black.

SCENE 9

Actors are seated:

1 Gandhi	4 Fart	6
2 Holly	5	
3 Condoleezza		

Fart—where'd she go?

Holly is dressed up like Larry King, and has adopted his manner-isms for the duration of this scene.

Holly/Larry: *And how long do you think this constipation will last?* That's the theme of tonight's episode. We have with us, via satellite from New Jersey, Condoleezza Rice, U.S. Secretary of State, and from modern India and, uh, Pakistan, Mahatma Mohandas Gan-dhi. And how long do you think this—constipation—will last? Ms. Rice?

Condoleezza: Well, Larry, do you mean how we talk past each other, never quite knowing what the other is saying—never quite knowing what we mean to each other, and to ourselves? Convinced only of our solitude, but chained by a dark gravity to the imperfect communion of speech?

Holly/Larry: Mr. Gandhi, thank you for being so patient.

Gandhi: I must, must take issue with the view of Ms. Rice. There is nothing in the data to suggest that I am the root of this prob-lem, nor can I accept the theory that a childhood trauma involving language is at the base of my interests in a unified theory of new media.

Condoleezza: This is—if you'll excuse me—an exact case in point. Mr. G., uh, the Mahatma, is not facing the truth that this adminis-tration has faced over and over again—the necessity to remain firm and clear-sighted in the cause of justice, to act determinedly and confidently in the international sphere, to provide a beacon for all nations to follow on the path toward democracy and freedom. (beat) This constipation cannot last.

Holly/Larry: Go Condoleezza!

Black.

Scene 10
Actors seated as in Scene 4.

Four people enter from the left side of the stage: Ezra Pound (very old), Diane Sawyer, Michael Palin as Jesus, John Malkovich, Poppy Brandes.

Ezra Pound: I'm Ezra Pound, rabid anti-Semite.

Diane Sawyer: I'm Diane Sawyer.

Jesus: (English accent, steps forward) Jesus, Son of God! (quick wave, steps back)

John Malkovich: (irate) I'M JOHN MALKOVICH WHAT THE FUCK IS THIS!?!

Poppy: I'm Poppy, Brian's landlord. (giggles)

Music starts—some kind of really trashy, "up" disco-funk. Everyone slowly, but then hectically, starts to break into a dance, including the four who were seated. Soon, the stage is filled with dancing figures. Ezra Pound is really beginning to cut a rug—just as he jumps into the air to click his heels—

Black.

SCENE 11

Actors are seated as before, except for Fart, who is standing by the stairs leading to Pétomane's "throne." Gandhi and Condoleezza are playing Trivial Pursuit.

Gandhi: Kashmir.

Fart: (makes slight raspberry sound)

Condoleezza: No, Lubeck!

Gandhi: Shit. Ok, category?

Condoleezza: Sports and Cryogenics.

Gandhi: Which legendary Boston Red Sox—

Condoleezza: Ted Williams!

Fart: (more, slightly weightier, raspberry)

They both turn toward Fart, with some look of hope on their faces. Fart looks like he is trying very hard to get another raspberry out. Pétomane's silhouette shifts accordingly with Fart as he is trying to do this.

166

Gandhi and Condoleezza finally realize that it's a false alarm.

Gandhi: (slapping card down) It's Ted Williams! Shit, Condi!

Condoleezza: (pumped) Yeess!

Black.

SCENE 12
Fart is standing where he was last scene. Other actors are seated:

1 Gandhi	4 Condoleezza	6
2	5 Holly	
3		

Condoleezza: (earnest) But—but I'm the first female African American United States Secretary of State!

Holly: (deadly, to audience) Go America.

Black.

SCENE 13
Middle two chairs have been removed. Holly is lying on the floor, on her back, asleep. Stage right is Fart, where he was last scene. Stage left, in the shadows, are Gandhi and Condoleezza. They start up a chant, quiet at first but then much louder:

Gandhi and Condoleezza:
Sea weed ketch-up.
Sea weed ketch-up.
Sea weed ketch-up.
Sea weed ketch-up.
Sea weed ketch-up.
Sea weed ketch-up.

Holly is having nightmares. They are of a horrific and sexual kind—think Rosemary's Baby. By the end of the next set of chants her groans are very loud.

Gandhi and Condoleezza:
Ki-wi pork chop.
Ki-wi pork chop.

Ki-wi pork chop.
Ki-wi pork chop.
Ki-wi pork chop.
Ki-wi pork chop.

Holly is in the throes of ecstasy or fear. The chant gets much faster:

Gandhi and Condoleezza:
Tofutti Cuties!
Tofutti Cuties!
Tofutti Cuties!
Tofutti Cuties!
Tofutti Cuties!
Tofutti Cuties!

Suddenly, Fart lets a out a big one, silencing the chant. As he does so, Pétomane shifts around uncomfortably—but relieved—in his seat.

Fart: Bloufuuhfhhfhghhhhffff!

Holly wakes up—huh?

Black.

Scene 14
Actors are seated:
1 Gandhi   4   6
2   5 Holly
3 Condoleezza

Fart is as before. He is simply going on, quite magisterially, with the longest, most various-sounding bout of flatulence in history—it's like sound poetry. Gandhi and Condoleezza are playing Scrabble.

Condoleezza: (triumphantly, putting down word) "Headroom."

Gandhi: Headroom! Headroom! That's not a word! That's not a word! That's—that's—hippyspeak! Hippyspeak! You have it in your country—but we clean the gutters in ours.

Condoleezza: Hippie-speak!

Gandhi: It's slang, Condi, it's slang. You used a slang word. There is

168

no headroom in English English. Or in Indian English. We must— (grandly) get thee to a dictionary!

Condoleezza: (unconcerned) Triple letter on the H, triple letter on the M, double word on the R. And it's Scrabble—all seven letters. One hundred seven points.

Gandhi: Headroom! Headroom!

Condoleezza: Headroom, Mr. G. It's the way the people talk—it's not in the dictionary. Language changes. Get used to "headroom"— it'll be around. If I have any say in the matter!

Gandhi: Headroom. (head in hands) Oy vey!

Black.

SCENE 15

All same as in last scene. Both players intensely concentrating.

Pétomane: (whimpering) Merde! Merrrrde!

Pause.

Condoleezza: Flutist of the anus! Hrumph!

Gandhi: (correcting her) Rectum.

Condoleezza: Rectum! (to herself) Asshole. (suddenly discovers the words in her letters) "Asshole"! (grandly puts the word on the board)

Gandhi groans.

Suddenly, there is a rhythmic variation in Fart's expulsion that catches their attention. They both turn suddenly toward Fart, who has gone silent. Fart himself doesn't quite know what's happened— he looks embarrassed.

He then repeats that same rhythmic phrase, with a slight melody. It is the opening notes to the French National Anthem. (Perhaps a cello playing the theme as it approaches in Tchaikovsky's 1812 Overture.) Pétomane wiggles his behind in time with the rhythm:

Fart: Plggh-plggh plggh-plggh plg plg plfg pflggggh plfjg plfjg—

169

Gandhi and Condoleezza are getting excited. Holly also notices what is happening and goes over.

Fart: Plggh-plggh plggh-plggh plg plg plfg pflggggh plfjg plfjg—

They are getting really excited. Suddenly, Fart sings, in a rich, triumphant baritone and a perfect, crisp French accent:

Fart: Allons! Enfants de la Patrie!
Le jour de gloire est arrivé!
Contre nous de la tyrannie,
L'étendard sanglant est levé!
Entendez-vous dans les campagnes
Mugir ces féroces soldats?
Ils viennent jusque dans vos bras
Égorger vos fils, vos compagnes.
Aux armes, citoyens!

Pétomane wiggles accordingly throughout this—very happy. Everybody claps, and give Fart a few congratulatory slaps on the shoulder—though get a little squeamish when they realize what they are doing. Le Pétomane appears from the waist up out the right side of the screen. He is wearing a blue beret and a red and white striped undershirt with long sleeves. He gives a "yay" gesture with two fists in the air.

Pétomane: Allors! I am cured! Viva la France! Viva la France! I am 'elty again!

Everybody claps, excited, except Holly.

Gandhi: Yes, and finally, finally, India will be free! We will be one nation, free from the yoke of foreign occupation! Free from the internal strife that keeps us a people divided! A nation of peace—and of language!

Ditto with the clapping.

Condoleezza: Yes, we have our voice back! We have our voice back! Our borders are secure! The singular moral voice of U.S. foreign policy will be the beacon of hope for the world. Freedom and democracy will reign supreme!

Ditto with the clapping. After clapping dies—

Holly: (deadly, to audience) Go America. (returns to her seat in the middle)

Pétomane: Oui! and France—and France—ma belle!—will be returned to its rightful place as ze capital of ze artistic world for the 21st century! Once again, France will be a strong nation—Paris will be ze, uh, Paris of Europe—ze Athens of, uh, ze Europe—for all eternity!

Ditto with the clapping.

Condoleezza: Ok, now pull your pants up and get your hairy ass out here so we can rehearse.

Pétomane disappears behind screen again. Gandhi and Condoleezza return to their chairs, begin to clear away Scrabble game from Pétomane's seat.

A head peeps out from stage right. It is plump face with big hairy moustache, and wearing a Prussian style military helmet with a spike on it. Soon, the man—it is Otto von Bismarck—appears in full, dressed in military regalia. He strides over to the free seat facing Holly.

Bismarck: (putting hand on back of chair) Ist dieser Platz frei?

Rutherford, Annandale, New York City, Providence,
Philadelphia, Querétaro, Mexico City, Los Angeles, Paris

BRIAN KIM STEFANS teaches literature and new media studies at UCLA. His current projects include a theory of digital textuality based on his series Third Hand Plays written for the SFMoma blog, a tentative foray into Speculaive Realist poetics, an historical anthology of Los Angeles poetry and Scavenged Luxury, an online "freeware" anthology of Los Angeles post-punk from roughly 1977-87. He lives in Hollywood.